WATCHMAN:
THE HALLMARKS

MASTERING YOUR CALLING AND MINISTRY

I0149585

DAMOLA TREASURE OKENLA

HILLTOP
Creative Publishers
PUSHING OUT THE MESSAGE FROM WITHIN

www.damolatreasureokenla.com

Okenla, Damola Treasure, 1966 –

Watchman: The Hallmarks

Mastering your calling and ministry

Dominique Lambright, Editor

Dawn James (Publish and Promote), Book Production

Kingdom Branding, Book Cover Design & Interior Layout

ISBN (Paperback) 978-1-948971-04-1

ISBN (eBook) 978-1-948971-05-8

Note to the reader: This book is not intended to dispense religious advice. The information is provided for educational and inspirational purposes only. In the event, you use any of the information in this book for yourself, which is your constitutional right, the author and publisher assumes no responsibility for your actions. In some chapters, names and locations have been changed to protect privacy.

Printed and bound in the United States

Praise for The Watchman: The Hallmarks

"Another excellent book by Pastor Damola Treasure Okenla, full of insights and empowerment principles for everyone to engage and triumph in the place of prayer."

~Pastor Yinka Adeyemo
RCCG, House on the Rock, Memphis TN

"I will recommend this book for anyone called as a watchman. The author gave deep insight to the ethics expected of any watchman 'green or seasoned' that wants to make the best of his or her calling, and also to please Him who has called him or her."

~Aderonke Akpoduado
Redeemed Christian Church of God
Jesus House Chicago, Watchmen Ministry

"This work is not only well laid out, but instructional and scriptural based. Her anecdotal style makes this book practical as she gives voice to different facets of intercession and roles of those called to prayer as watchmen."

~Pastor Sandra Howell
New Life Church Southeast

"In the middle ages, watchmen were tasked with keeping a watch over a city to prevent enemy attacks. In this book, the author uses the concept of the watchman to provide insight into this important, but often neglected calling. I would recommend this book to anyone who is committed to mastering the ministry of a watchman: a defender, warrior, prophet, counselor, intercessor."

~ Olu A Adesida
Consultant

DEDICATION:
WATCHMAN: THE HALLMARKS

To God, the Father, the Son, and the Holy Spirit for making this possible, and to all the wonderful men and women of God with whom I have watched and am still watching over the church of God, Cities, and families. (RCCG HOUSE OF GRACE, LAGOS NIGERIA,1999 - 2003, RCCG JESUS HOUSE CHICAGO, 2004 - 2016, LIFE ENCOUNTERS OUTREACHES; TRANSFORMATIONAL PRAYERS NETWORK, Since 2007 to datet)

You have all been wonderful instruments in advancing the Kingdom.

ACKNOWLEDGMENTS

I would like to acknowledge and appreciate the people whom God used to enhance and establish my calling as a watchman, my Pastors, and mentors and starting with my most recent Pastor, Pastor Adebayo Adewole of RCCG Jesus House Chicago, Pastor Babs Ajayi of the then, RCCG House of Grace, Lagos, Pastor Ibukun Williams then of RCCG Grace Tabernacle Lagos.

I would also like to appreciate Pastor Yinka Adeyemo of RCCG House On the Rock Memphis of whose Church I first taught the contents of this book in April 2010.

And to all Pastors whom I have also taught the contents of this book in their church, I'm most grateful to you for opening your doors for me.

I say thank you to everyone who worked on this book and Mrs. Grace Oluwaseun Adelegan-Olaleye and Phillip Adelegan for collating my notes.

Once again to God be all the glory!

CONTENTS

WHY THIS BOOK: THE HALLMARK OF A WATCHMAN

Those who have identified themselves as watchmen and have responded to that identity, that they may know how to do the work effectively.

For those who are yet to identify themselves, that they may discover who they are and know how to do the work effectively.

"So you, my son, be strong [constantly strengthened] and empowered in the grace that is [to be found only] in Christ Jesus. The things [the doctrine, the precepts, the admonitions, the sum of my ministry] which you have heard me teach in the presence of many witnesses, entrust [as a treasure] to reliable and faithful men who will also be capable and qualified to teach others." (2 Timothy 2:1-2)

- For us to understand what it means to be a watchman in today's context as compared to the biblical days.

- We need to instruct the new entrants the ropes, so they don't become a casualty of spiritual warfare, because we are spiritual soldiers in the LORD's army. Just like we have casualties of war in the physical sense, we have spiritual warfare. We have soldiers wounded and who never recover from their wound to continue in the battlefield. Believe me, as a watchman you are not immune to attacks. The Devil does not attack what has no potential. As a Christian, you are already on his list, and to crown it you enlisted in a special list. That is why you must play according to the rules of the game.

"Take with me your share of hardship [passing through the difficulties which you are called to endure], like a good soldier of Christ Jesus. No soldier in active service gets entangled in the [ordinary business] affairs of civilian life; [he avoids them] so that he may please the one who enlisted him to serve." (2 Timothy 2:3-4)

- For the watchmen to avoid errors and misconceptions that can come with ministry.

"Pay close attention to yourself [concentrate on your personal development] and to your teaching; persevere in these things [hold to them], for as you do this you will ensure salvation both for yourself and for those who hear you." (1 Timothy 4:16)

- To encourage the watchmen. There is something for the greens and the seasoned. It is a refresher course.

INTRODUCTION:
THE HALLMARK OF A WATCHMAN

Every individual or group in their existence has at least a time when they face a trial or trials that look overwhelming, and things may continue to go wrong and spiral uncontrollably downward if something is not done quickly.

At a church where I was a co-pastor at between the year 1999 and 2003, I observed those challenges that make men quit their calling and even place of assignment due to not knowing what to do, or how to go about what they know how to do. Ministers left, workers left, and in my plan to also leave, a fellow minister and a parish pastor encouraged me not to move, but instead join his own prayer group on Tuesdays to pray for my pastor and the church. I obliged to this kind gesture, and I continued with them for some time, until a day I heard in my spirit, "I have appointed you a watchman over my church, and I will raise others along with you." That was when I was led to the verse in Isaiah 62:6-7. Hitherto, even though I have been involved in the prayer groups since 1989, I had never heard of the word WATCHMAN. I'd been used to words like prayer warriors, prayer champions, and intercessors at most. I have attended a prayer school, but I never heard that particular word, watchman, used to describe people who pray.

With this new development and zeal, I ran back to my church, and with the courtesy of my pastor, I announced to invite those who thought they were called to pray for the church. My mistake! No further prayer, no inquiries from God to know the right people. First, people came but were wrong for the job. Lesson learned: not everyone that poses to pray for the church are actually interested, but instead have other mindsets. I prayed again, and God showed me who should be involved; they came, and till I left that church in 2003 I prayed along with this set of people every Tuesday night. No more than seven people, about six men with my very self as the only woman. Things turned around for better for the church.

In my relocation to the US, I moved into a new parish of the same church by September 2003, and God revealed things glorious things about the future of the church and the hindrances too, some of which I'd shared with no one. There is always an appointed time to reveal things, and some will never be, but the manifestations for God's glory cannot be shared.

As God would have His way, my appointment to lead the prayer ministry of the church was in July 2004, a post I held till July 2016; except for a year sabbatical to serve in another area of the ministry due to need.

With the passion and the calling, I wanted to turn everybody into a watchman. I met several resistances until I heard the Spirit of God speak to me, "You cannot make people become what I have not made them to be." So, I soft-pedaled to work with what I had. I'm still praying that God will raise watchmen for his church.

Often because of my experience with the people in the prayer ministry and learning from my own mistakes, I had wanted to put things down to help others. But the inspiration to write this instruction book did not come until March 2010, exactly March 16th at 5:00 in the morning, just as I was getting up, I heard in my spirit, "Mark of a successful watchman." The ethics were dictated to me by the Holy Spirit.

Shortly after, I had to do a three-day program for a church, and the prayer team asked me to meet with them, especially for a session on a Saturday morning. While there with them, as I was thinking of what to teach, I was reminded of the note. Still, in a raw form, I spoke from the heart.

Thank God for the crisis in House of Grace for bringing the aspect of me as a Watchman and thank God for the opportunity Jesus House Chicago afforded me to do what I know how to do best. I am still discovering more since I am still in the school of experience and teaching by the Holy Spirit.

To do this, there has been so many life challenging issues, but I thank God I can put it down and I hope somebody can learn from them.

CHAPTER 1

WHO IS A WATCHMAN?
THE PERSON OF A WATCHMAN

"Who rises from prayer a better man, his prayer is answered." - George Meredith

SCRIPTURE:

"I've posted watchmen on your walls, Jerusalem. Day and night they keep at it, praying, calling out, and reminding God to remember. They are to give him no peace until he does what he said, until he makes Jerusalem famous as the City of Praise". (Isaiah 62:6-7)

The word "WATCHMEN", comes from the Hebrew word 'tsaphah' meaning to lean forward, to peer into, the distance, to observe, to behold, to spy, to wait for.

A Watchman is that person that has been appointed by God to watch over the performance of His promise for a place or over a people. The Watchman will, therefore, be a person that has had insight into the will of God and carefully by prayer keeps observing by taking a look and keeping attention towards the fulfillment of the promise. He keeps a lookout for the appearance or happenings to usher in the promise.

The watchmen I have discovered over time can be positioned over families, Churches, cities, and nations; or over a project or a cause.

One of my earliest pictures of a watchman is from my growing up years; then we had the main building outside a gatehouse manned by several watchmen/gate men who took turns to watch the building day and the night, armed with Dane gun (a locally made flintlock musket). While everybody else stays in-doors, they stay outside. If there is trouble, they blow whistles.

"Green Shoot will sprout from Jesse's stump, from his roots a budding Branch. The life-giving Spirit of God will hover over him, the Spirit that brings wisdom and understanding, The Spirit that gives direction and builds strength, the Spirit that instills knowledge and Fear-of-God.

Fear-of-God will be all his joy and delight. He won't judge by appearances, won't decide based on hearsay. He'll judge the needy by what is a right; render decision on earth's poor with justice.

His words will bring everyone to awed attention. A mere breath from his lips will topple the wicked. Each morning he'll pull on sturdy work clothes and boots and build righteousness and faithfulness in the land." (Isaiah 11:1-5)

The above was the prophecy about the birth of Jesus as the Messiah for Israel as promised by God and foretold by prophet Isaiah, but some people took it upon themselves to birth the prophecy in the place of prayer.

Examples of such are people like Simeon and Anna as recorded in the book of Luke.

"In Jerusalem at the time, there was a man, Simeon by name, a good man, a man who lived in the prayerful expectancy of help for Israel. And the Holy Spirit was on him. The Holy Spirit had shown him that he would see the Messiah of God before he died. Led by the Spirit, he entered the Temple. As the parents of the child Jesus brought him in to carry out the rituals of the Law, Simeon took him into his arms and blessed God: God, you can now release your servant; release me in peace as you promised. With my own eyes, I've seen your salvation; it's now out in the open for everyone to see:

A God-revealing light to the non-Jewish nations, and of glory for your people Israel. Jesus' father and mother were speechless with surprise at these words. Simeon blessed them and said to Mary, his mother.

"This child marks both the failure and the recovery of many

in Israel, A figure misunderstood and contradicted— The pain of a sword-thrust through you. But the rejection will force honesty, as God reveals who they really are." (Luke 2:25-35)

"Anna the prophetess was also there, a daughter of Phanuel from the tribe of Asher. She was by now a very old woman. She had been married seven years and a widow for eighty-four. She never left the Temple area, worshiping night and day with her fasting and prayers. At the very time Simeon was praying, she showed up, broke into an anthem of praise to God, and talked about the child to all who were waiting expectantly for the freeing of Jerusalem." (Luke 2:36-38)

Those two were in the know of the purpose and will of God for Israel and carefully followed the trends of happenings, observing the unfolding of a promise of the Messiah. They both monitored the events leading to the birth of Christ, making sure they did not miss it when it happened.

As one can observe from the words of Simeon that which was secret is now out in the open for everyone to see. What the watchman knows and sees may not be open to everybody, even though it is written, it is divinely revealed and given understanding too, by the Holy Spirit to whoever God has purposed to use.

This is GOD's Word on the subject: *"As soon as Babylon's seventy years are up and not a day before, I'll show up and take care of you as I promised and bring you back home. I know what I'm doing. I have it all planned out—plans to take care of you, not abandon you, plans to give you the future you hope for. "When you call on me, when you come and pray to me, I'll listen. "When you come looking for me, you'll find me. "Yes, when you get serious about finding me and want it more than anything else, I'll make sure you won't be disappointed." GOD's Decree. "I'll turn things around for you. I'll bring you back from all the countries into which I drove you"—GOD's Decree—"bring you home to the place from which I sent you off into exile. You can count on it." (Jeremiah 29:10-14)*

Yes, God had planned for the freedom of Israel from Babylon, but it would not have happened if nobody would pray it through. Such came in the person of Daniel.

"Darius, son of Ahasuerus, born a Mede, became king over the land of Babylon. In the first year of his reign, I, Daniel, was meditating on the Scriptures that gave, according to the Word of God to the prophet Jeremiah, the number of years that Jerusalem had to lie in ruins, namely, seventy. I turned to the Master God, asking for an answer—praying earnestly, fasting from meals, wearing rough penitential burlap, and kneeling in the ashes. I poured out my heart, baring my soul to God, my God." (Daniel 9:1-3)

The overdue stay of the Hebrew children in the land of Egypt would probably be due to the absence of anyone, observing, and monitoring events towards fulfilling the promise of freedom.

"GOD said to Abram, "Know this: your descendants will live as outsiders in a land, not theirs; they'll be enslaved and beaten down for 400 years. Then I'll punish their slave masters; your offspring will march out of there loaded with plunder. But not you; you'll have a long and full life and die a good and peaceful death. Not until the fourth generation will your descendants return here; sin is still a thriving business among the Amorites." (Genesis. 15: 13-16)

'Then Joseph died, and all his brothers—that whole generation. But the children of Israel kept on reproducing. They were very prolific—a population explosion in their own right—and the land was filled with them.

A new king came to power in Egypt who didn't know Joseph. He spoke to his people in alarm, "There are way too many of these Israelites for us to handle. We've got to do something: Let's devise a plan to contain them, lest if there's a war they should join our enemies, or just walk off and leave us.

So, they organized them into work-gangs and put them to hard labor under gang-foremen. They built the storage cities Pithom and Rameses for Pharaoh. But the harder the Egyptians worked them the more children the Israelites had—children everywhere! The Egyptians got so they couldn't stand the Israelites and treated them worse than ever, crushing them with slave labor. They made them miserable with hard labor—making bricks and mortar and back-breaking work in the fields. They piled on the work, crushing them under the cruel workload."

(Exodus 1:6-14)

Nothing happens except someone prays; the watchman will pray through to bring to pass the promise of God.

THE CONCEPT OF THE WATCHMAN IN THE OLD TESTAMENT AND THE NEW TESTAMENT

- The Watchman in the Old Testament stands for guards, lookouts, and sentries. Primarily the watchman is expected to look out for trouble and make reports about what they see. (2 Samuel 18:24-27)

- The Watchmen were professionals who could discern messenger of war or peace from afar. In the New Testament version, the watchman is expected to watch out for infiltration of false teachings and doctrines. Importation of strange gods into a community. The watchmen will pray for exposure of such people and revival. (2 Peter 2:1-2; Acts 20:28-31)

- In their looking out they observed and sensed imminent trouble. (2 Kings 9:17 -18)

- The watchmen warn the people on behalf of God. (Ezekiel 3:17; 33:2, 6-7)

- The watchmen look out for the enemy and warn the people. Whenever there was the approach of danger, they sound the alarm.

- God appoints the Watchman or places a burden in the heart of a person about His will and purpose for a nation or a people (Ezekiel 3:17)

- The will and purpose of God revealed to the Watchman by the Holy Spirit through meditation of the word or by a direct revelation (Ezekiel 37:1; 1 Corinthians 2:9-12)

- The Watchman is expected to pray through into manifestation the will and purpose of God. It is very important to know the will of God concerning the place or people for without the knowledge of that will be fruitless to engage in prayer; just like Daniel knew what to pray concerning Israel in the book of Daniel chapter 9 with revelation from Jeremiah 29: 11-14

- The Watchman must be able to see from God's perspective, that is the kingdom's view. You cannot pray by following the popular opinion of men, but by God's will and plan. (Isaiah 55:9-11)

- The watchman must be able to declare to the people on behalf of God. That also means you must spend much more time in the presence of God. I always say you don't have the right to speak to the people of God without first speaking to the God of the people. (Isaiah 21:6)

- The promise, purpose, and plans of God have a time frame for the manifestation failure to discern this divine timing will cause delay. You must be patient to pray through. Apostle Paul once said in Galatians 4:19. *"My little children, for whom I travail or labor in birth again until Christ is formed in you."* The watchman is a patient laborer or traveler. (2 Peter 3:9)

- The Watchman is expected to observe events, keep looking out for appearances and situations. Don't be suspicious, but be discerning. Don't be spiritually clueless about happenings in your environment. Being spiritually blind, deaf or dumb is dangerous. (Isaiah 42)

- The Watchman monitors the progression of the fulfillment with the view of protecting it from derailment, and diversions.

- The Watchman keeps calling on God relentlessly to remind Him of His promise until actualization.

- The watchman prays through until something happens. Prays until there is a desired result.

- The Watchman is expected to know what he has to pray through for. This could be the godly vision given at the beginning of a local church and additional prophecies over time, the promise of God for a nation including past prophecies and new ones. The plan and purpose of God for an individual or a family.

- The appointment of a Watchman is usually over a territory or over a sphere of influence.

- It is not a call for the slothful because it requires hard work.

- A Watchman is a man of purpose. Prays "Let thy will be done," that is the will of God in contrast to the will of man.

- The watchman work over time.

- God is ready to listen to the Watchman.

- The Watchman acts in divine partnership with God.

- In the kingdom, nothing happens except man prays.

- To fulfill his role, he serves in a different capacity.

HOW TO BECOME A WATCHMAN

It is a calling like any other calling, and the calling is done by God. (Romans 8:30; 11:29; Galatians 1:6; Ephesians 4:1)

- It comes as a burden; when issues become heavy in your heart, you just want to see it solved. For example, you discover anytime you hear your pastor speak from the altar about an issue or project you develop a burden to pray for it until it is resolved; that may be a pointer to you calling. (Luke 10: 30-37; Galatians 6:1-10)

- Once you sense your calling, you must be active about it. If there is any constituted team already in your church, seek to join them for training and development.

- You must walk worthy of your calling doing everything possible to fulfill the calling. (Ephesians 4:1-2)

- Your calling could also be circumstantial, that is God can use your circumstance to actualize your call as a watchman. God can force a chosen vessel to become humble through affliction. (Leviticus 26:41) and that is why God said *"Behold, I have refined you, but not as silver; I have tried and chosen you in the furnace of affliction."* (Isaiah 48:10). Examples of such people that God chose but had to go through trials and hardship are Abraham (Genesis 18:27) Jacob (Genesis 32:10) Moses (Exodus 3:11) Joshua (Joshua 7:6) Gideon (Judge 6:15) David (1 Chronicle 29:14)

REFLECTIONS

- How well do you understand your calling? Are you clear or do you still need clarity?

- In what situation was God calling evident to you?

- What insight or action step has been laid in your heart now?

CHAPTER 2

THE POTENTIALS OF THE WATCHMAN

"When you catch a glimpse of your potential, that's when passion is born."- Zig Ziglar

SCRIPTURE:

"And [I pray] that the eyes of your heart [the very center and core of your being] may be enlightened [flooded with light by the Holy Spirit], so that you will know and cherish the hope [the divine guarantee, the confident expectation] to which He has called you, the riches of His glorious inheritance in the saints (God's people)." (Ephesians 1:18)

As a WATCHMAN, you have chances of playing and developing into many roles or parts to enhance and fulfill your calling.

These many parts will show up as you continue in the ministry. You will need to pay attention to know what area to focus on and develop to be more effective in the delivery of your service.

A DEFENDER

The imagery of walls and gates positioned the watchman to be on the defensive protecting people, places, and things from the enemy invasion. It can also be offensive by attacking the enemies at his gates and walls.

- The Watchman defends the body of Christ from the onslaught and distraction of the enemy on the body.

"Because it was our will to come to you. [I mean that] I, Paul, again and again [wanted to come], but Satan hindered and impeded us." (1 Thessalonians 2:18)

That was why Paul made a request for prayer. If evil is prevailing against the body or in the world, it means no people are praying or praying right.

- As a watchman, you are expected to defend the spreading of the word of God from hindrances.

- As a watchman, you are expected to be sensitive in the spirit and sound alarm of imminent spiritual attacks on the body of Christ.

- As a watchman, you are expected to defend the body of Christ as represented by any institution from ferocious attack.

One can observe from the scripture below, a request by a desperate pastor asking for prayers.

"Furthermore, brethren, do pray for us, that the Word of the Lord may speed on (spread rapidly and run its course) and be glorified (extolled) and triumph, even as [it has done] with you, And that we may be delivered from perverse (improper, unrighteous) and wicked (actively malicious) men, for not everybody has faith and is held by it." (2 Thessalonians 3:1-2)

- The watchman is expected to resist the devil on behalf of the people and places. "Resist the devil [stand firm against him], and he will flee from you." (James 4:7)

- To defend, you must be on alert, which is to be vigilant in the spirit and sometimes in the physical. That was why Paul advised, *"Pray at all times (on every occasion, in every season) in the Spirit, with all [manner of] prayer and entreaty. Keep alert and watch with strong purpose and perseverance, interceding in behalf of all the saints (God's consecrated people.)* (Ephesians 6:18)

"Be well balanced (temperate, sober of mind), be vigilant and cautious; for that enemy of yours, the devil, roams around like a lion roaring in fierce hunger], seeking someone to seize upon and devour. Withstand him; be firm in faith [against his onset—rooted, established, strong, immovable, and determined], knowing that the same identical

sufferings are appointed to your brotherhood (the whole body of Christians) throughout the world."(1 Peter 5: 8-9)

• You cannot afford to be careless or ignorant about spiritual matters. Or else not only will Satan take advantage of the people or the people you are to watch over but the possibility of you becoming a casualty of war is unavoidable. *"To keep Satan from getting the advantage over us; for we are not ignorant of his wiles and intentions."* (2 Corinthians 2:11)

• Sensitivity is very important in detecting and foiling the plans of the enemy. Therefore, the spiritual gift of discerning of spirit and words of knowledge is needful.

A WARRIOR

As a watchman, you will be expected to fight spiritual battles for the promise to come to manifestation. According to Paul in the book of Ephesians, there are battles, and they are not physical but spiritual.

"For we are not wrestling with flesh and blood [contending only with physical opponents], but against the despotisms, against the powers, against [the master spirits who are] the world rulers of this present darkness, against the spirit forces of wickedness in the heavenly (supernatural) sphere." (Ephesians 6:12)

As a soldier in the kingdom army, and as a watchman

you are expected to fight wars. The wars are not carnal but spiritual, therefore know how to fight spiritual warfare using spiritual weapons.

"For the weapons of our warfare are not physical [weapons of flesh and blood], but they are mighty before God for the overthrow and destruction of strongholds." (2 Corinthians 10:4)

A Watchman is mandated to destroy anything that can stand as an obstruction to the manifestation of the promise of God in any place, and in the lives of the people involved.

Any Pharaoh in our lives that has refused to let us go must perish. (Pharaoh was an obstruction to the promises of God for the Israelites; he was a stubborn pursuer despite several warnings, he still did not let the Israelites go until he drowned at the red sea.)

- The Watchman will also be expected to be involved in the repairs and reconstruction of broken walls.

"See, I have this day appointed you to the oversight of the nations and of the kingdoms to root out and pull down, to destroy and to overthrow, to build and to plant." (Jeremiah 1:10)

- In the execution of spiritual warfare, the Watchman becomes a battle axe in the hand of God. He is not by himself but an instrument in the hand of God.

"You [Cyrus of Persia, soon to conquer Babylon] are my battle-ax or maul and weapon of war--for with you I break nations in pieces, with you I destroy kingdoms." (Jeremiah 51:20)

- The watchman is not expected to give up fighting for the object of 'watch.' Or else the vision could be destroyed or hijacked by the enemy as buttressed by the scripture below:

"The mighty warriors of Babylon have ceased to fight; they have remained in their holds. Their might has failed; they have become [weak and helpless] like women. Her dwelling places are burned up; her bars [and defenses generally] are broken." (Jeremiah 51:30)

- It is a fight to the finish as it was described by Paul in Ephesians 6:12, and as explained by King Solomon:

"And that about wraps it up. God is strong, and he wants you strong. So, take everything the Master has set out for you, well-made weapons of the best materials. And put them to use so you will be able to stand up to everything the Devil throws your way. This is no afternoon athletic contest that we'll walk away from and forget about in a couple of hours. This is for keeps, a life-or-death fight to the finish against the Devil and all his angels."

"There is a purpose and there is a time for that purpose and a time to fight for the purpose. There is time for war and there is time for peace." (Ecclesiastes: 3:1-8)

- The watchmen are to battle against all kinds of opposition to the kingdom of God to ensure that the gates of Hades are not prevailing.

"We have wickedness in high places represented by kind of King Herod's; there was a Herod who rose against Jesus at birth (Matthew 2) and there was a Herod who rose against the Apostles (Acts 12) Pharaohs and Goliath who will not want the kingdom work to thrive. They are called 'the god of this world." (Psalm 2:8; 2 Corinthians 4:4, Zechariah 1:17-20)

- By spiritual warfare, the watchman enforces the victory won at the Calvary. God needs militant men and women on the battlefield. It is written:

"And from the days of John the Baptist until the present time, the kingdom of heaven has endured violent assault, and violent men seize it by force [as a precious prize--a share in the heavenly kingdom is sought with most ardent zeal and intense exertion]." (Matthew 11:12)

"Victory is an accomplished fact, but it does need a man to lay hold of that victory and precipitate a confrontation with the enemy and resist him.

Epaphras was a victory enforcer, and it was said of him; "Epaphras, who is one of you and a servant of Christ Jesus, sends greetings. He is always wrestling in prayer for you, that you may stand firm in all the will of God, mature and fully assured". (Colossians 4:12)

- There is a war, and that war is the war of faith.

"This charge and admonition I commit in trust to you, Timothy, my son, in accordance with prophetic intimations which I formerly received concerning you, so that inspired and aided by them you may wage the good warfare." (1 Timothy 1:18)

- The war is not a carnal one and therefore cannot be won with carnal methods. It is stated:

"For the weapons of our warfare are not physical [weapons of flesh and blood], but they are mighty before God for the overthrow and destruction of strongholds. (2 Corinthians 10:4)

Looking at the story of David and Goliath: Humanly speaking David would not have defeated Goliath on his own if not for God on his side.

- As believers, we have been appointed as soldiers in this war and much more as a watchman.

- In this warfare as a watchman, you have been given authority to tread on Satan and his kingdom (Luke 10:19, Jeremiah 1:10)

- We have been spiritually empowered for the battle ahead through the Holy Spirit. You are therefore not on your own. What Jesus promised the disciples still stands for us, *"Then I will ask the Father to send you the Holy Spirit who will help you and always be with you."* So, let us consider areas of Spiritual empowerment we have at our disposal through the Holy Spirit:

1. Spiritual identity: (Romans 8:14; 2 Timothy 2:4; Genesis 1:27; Jeremiah 1:5; John 1:12; 1 Corinthians 6:17; 1 Peter 2:9; Revelations 1:6)
2. Spiritual vision and insight: (2 Kings 6:17 20; Isaiah 42; Joel 2:28-29; Numbers 12:6; Ephesians 3:16-17; 1:18; Habakkuk 2:2-3; 2 Corinthians 12:1-4)
3. Spiritual guidance (Psalm 32:8; John 16:13; Isaiah 30:21; Psalm 119:105; John 14:26; Isaiah 58:11; Psalms 25:9-10; Leviticus 19:31; Isaiah 48:17)
4. Spiritual gifts (1 Corinthians 12:1-11; Romans 12:6-8)
5. Spiritual anointing (Luke 22:49; Isaiah 61:1-2; 11:1-3; Acts 10:38; Luke 4:18; Psalm 92:10; 1 John 2:2: 20, 27; Psalm 45:7; Exodus 28:41 Ezekiel 37:1; Psalm 23; Exodus 29:7; Psalm 89:10)
6. Spiritual strength (Joshua 1:9; Isaiah 40; Philippians 4:13; 2 Corinthians 12: 9-11)
7. Spiritual authority (Luke 10:19; 9:1 Colossians 2:9-10; Matthew 10:1; 1 John 4:4; 2 Corinthians 10:3-5)
8. Spiritual Protection (1 John 5:4-5; Deuteronomy 28:7; Jeremiah 1:17-19; Joshua 1:1-8; Ephesians 6:13; 1 Peter 5:8)

A PROPHET

A Watchman often also performs the role of a prophet. This is not surprising since he is expected to hear from God to speak and act.

"The Sovereign Lord never does anything without revealing his plan to his servants, the prophets." (Amos 3:7)

WHAT IS PROPHECY?

Prophecy is a Hebrew word "MASSA," meaning "to prophesy a burden or to declare an utterance."

- The watchman as a prophet interprets the divine will of God. For a Watchman to play the role of prophet, he/she must be able to hear from God. And He said hear now my words:

  "If there is a prophet among you, I the Lord make myself known to him in a vision and speak to him in a dream." (Numbers 12:6; Deuteronomy 18:17)

- A watchman that wants to prosper in ministry must know how the prophetic ministry operates to avoid error. There is a spirit of prophecy (1 Corinthians 12:10), and there is a gift of prophecy (Romans 12:6), and there is the office of the prophet. (Ephesians 4:11)

- Prophecy is more than divine inspiration or even revelation. True prophecy is the ability to accurately perceive and proclaim present spiritual realities and to prepare for the future.

- Prophecy is the unveiling of the heart, purposes, and will of God to His people or given to an individual, family, community, and a nation.

- Prophecy is output and prophet is a person. It can be very personal, but private or public like the one Timothy had of which Paul reminded him of (1 Timothy 1:18-19)

- Prophecy is used by God for the deliverance, healing, and restoration of His people. (Hosea 12:13)

- Prophecy offers hope and strength to God's people.

- Prophecy is used for empowering and equipping God's people to fulfill their divine purpose, call, and destiny.

- Prophecy is also described as the "Word of the Lord". You often hear Prophet Ezekiel starting his message with, "The Word of the Lord came to me." (Ezekiel 1:3; 2 Thessalonians 3:1)

The Purpose of Prophecy

- To exalt Jesus. (Revelation 19:10; John 16:14; Philippians 2:9-10])

- To receive verbal communication from God in our own known languages. (1 Corinthians 14:2 -3; 2 Peter 1 :19,21)

- To give vocal expression to other spiritual gifts, for example, the gift of words of knowledge and that of the words of wisdom need the prophetic anointing for their expression to the body of

Christ. The gift of power, for the most part, needs the gift of prophecy for the articulation of their manifestations.

- To build the Church.

- The gift of prophecy that operates beside the office of the prophet is meant for the edification, comfort, and exhortation. (1 Corinthians 14:3)

Today it works through Spirit-filled believers and spoken through:

- Prophetic Teaching

- Office of the Prophet

- Prophetic Preaching

- The Gift of Prophecies

- Prophetic Music

- Prophetic Prayers

- Prophetic Declaration of the Scriptures

The Watchman and Prophecy

- The Watchman as prophet predicts or foretells the future; an example is Elijah. (2 King 7)

- The Watchman as a prophet promotes godly causes and ideas. (2 Chronicles.15:8)

- The Watchman as a prophet is used by God to warn His people of:

1. An impending danger from the enemy. And for them to keep off danger. (Jeremiah 51:2; Nehemiah 4:9; Isaiah 21:8)
2. The Watchman is expected to be on alert to report the approach of the enemy (2 Samuel.18:24-27; 2 Kings 9:17 -20; Isaiah 21:6; 7-9; Jeremiah 6:16-17; 2 Samuel 18:26; 2 Kings 9:17; Ezekiel 33:2-3; 2 Kings 6:8-12; Daniel 4:17)

- God's impending judgment against them for forsaking His ways.

- The Watchman as a prophet is used by God to call out for repentance. (Jeremiah 31:6)

- The Watchman as prophet anticipates victory. (Isaiah 52:8)

For a Watchman to prosper in the ministry of a prophet, it would be very needful to operate in the gift of the Spirit known as the revelation gifts. These gifts are; words of wisdom, words of knowledge discerning of spirit and prophecy.

"To one is given in and through the [Holy] Spirit [the power to speak] a message of wisdom, and to another [the power to express] a word of knowledge and understanding according to the same [Holy] Spirit; To another wonder-working] faith by the same [Holy] Spirit, to another the extraordinary powers of healing by the one Spirit; To another the working of miracles, to another prophetic insight the gift of interpreting the divine will and

*purpose); to another the ability to discern and distinguish between [the utterances of true] spirits [and false ones], to another various kinds of [unknown] tongues, to another the ability to interpret [such] tongues." (*1 Corinthians 12:8-10)

How is information revealed to a Prophet?

God is the source of the prophetic message, and human vessels become the channel for relaying that message to the people concerned.

Information can be revealed to a prophet through the Holy Spirit in different ways. These ways could be through:

Prayers (Acts 13:2-4)

Praise: (Acts 13:1-4; 2 Chronicles 20)

The Word: studying and meditating. (Psalm 119:105; Hebrews 1:2; Psalm 25:4)

Vivid Dreams. (Job 33:14 17)

Direct communication. (Numbers 12:6-8)

Open Visions. (Acts 9:8; 10:1-3;9-10; 11:13-14 16: 6-10)

Voice of the Spirit. (Psalm 29; John 1:1; Romans 8:14)

Witness of the Spirit. (Acts 8:29; 10:19; 11:12; John 16:13)

Through impressions or a knowing: Sudden thought about someone or something. You will hear people say something like, "It was impressed upon my spirit or I perceived." (Acts 14:9; 27:10; 27: 22-25)

Mental picture or spiritual impression or perception.

How to interpret the information revealed.

Before information is declared, the watchman must be able to ascertain that the information has been declared to the right people and that they are ready to accept the information.

Words of wisdom

This is a divine revelation of the plan and purpose of God, given a specific situation or instance. It gives a directive on what to do. It proffers a solution, an example is the case of Joseph interpretation of Pharaoh's dream {Genesis 41] and Paul and the crew in Acts 27. It offers solutions to the issues exposed by the Word of Knowledge.

Words of knowledge

Reveals the specific facts about a person, place, or event. It includes name, history, current issues, which ordinarily is unknown to the speaker, but revealed by the spirit of God. A classic example is Jesus' encounter with the woman by the well. (John 4:16-19) it diagnoses foundational issues and solutions.

Discerning of Spirits

It means the ability to distinguish between two or more things. In this regard between the Holy and Evil spirit, Godly and ungodly spirit. Insight into a given situation. Awareness of purpose and presence, an example is the story of Saul's encounter with the young girl who was a sorcerer in Acts 16.

"She kept following Paul and [the rest of] us, shouting loudly, these men are the servants of the Most High God! They announce to you the way of salvation! And she did this for many days. Then Paul, being sorely annoyed and worn out, turned and said to the spirit within her, I charge you in the name of Jesus Christ to come out of her! And it came out that very [a]moment." (Acts 16:17-18)

It's to know how information is revealed, how to interpret, and how to apply.

There are three sources of revelation: The Holy Spirit, the devil, and self. The watchman to be sure of the source, confirm with the word of God. We were instructed in (1 John 4:1) not to believe every spirit but that every spirit should be subjected to test to know whether they are of God.

Revelations are not to boost the Watchman ego but to feed the prayers. Some information is just privileged kingdom information needful to carry out the kingdom assignment on the altar of prayer. Often, to show off, we hear and we rush to tell.

- Before you declare any information, you must inquire from God the recipient, the way and time of delivery.

- Distinguish between your voice and other voices. When Paul got his call, he knew it was the Lord's voice. (Acts 22:7) according to Paul, there may be so many kinds of voices in the world, and none of them is without significance. (1 Corinthians 14:10)

- Do not be carried away in your meetings by so much of prophecy. Test every prophecy including yours. (1 John 4: 1-2)

- Do not despise prophecy, so often because we have no particular gift we condemn and criticize those who have. (1 Thessalonians 5:19-21;1 Corinthians 14:26 - 33)

- Prophecy should seek to edify, exhort and comfort not to tear down or discourage others. (1 Corinthians 14:3)

LIMITATIONS

- Lack of adequate knowledge about prophecy by the watchman and the fact that as human we are limited, unlike God who is Omniscient and who as a custodian of knowledge can decide on what He would want us to know in time. (1 Corinthians 13:9; Daniel 2:21-23])

- Level of faith (Romans 12:6)

- Level of maturity (1 Corinthians 3: 1-3)

- Conflict of interest and personal biases will disrupt the flow of information to you. You have to be far away from Church politics and preferences. (1 Corinthians 3:4 -9)

- The watchman experiences.

- Personality of the watchman.

COUNSELOR /ADVISOR

As a Watchman, you would be expected to sometime play the role of a counselor on issues such as personal, social, spiritual, or psychological to the leaders and the people under your spiritual influence. Just like Samuel unto Saul and David, we also saw the part prophet Nathan played in the story of David and Bathsheba, the wisdom and the etiquette of delivery and on the Solomon as the King instead of Adonijah. (2 Samuel 12) Prophet Isaiah was a counselor to King Hezekiah during reign as king (Isaiah 37:2-3), and Zechariah was to Uzziah "He set himself to seek God in the days of Zechariah, who instructed him in the things of God; and as long as he sought (inquired of, yearned for) the Lord, God made him prosper." (2 Chronicles 26:5)

Leaders need spiritual support from the watchman. As the watchman stands in gap for the leaders and is able to hear from God, he could communicate such in the form of counsel to such a leader; with all humility and wisdom, you better learn from Prophet Nathan.

"Where no wise guidance is, the people fall, but in the multitude of counselors there is safety." (Proverbs 11:14)

"For by wise counsel you can wage your war, and in an abundance of counselors there is victory and safety" (Proverbs 24:6)

AN INTERCESSOR

By your calling as a Watchman, you would also play the role of an intercessor.

WHAT IS INTERCESSION?

- Intercession is the act of standing between the need that is seen, and the provision required. It can cover an individual, a people, a church, a city, and a nation. God himself announced his desperate need for someone to stand in the gap for the land.

"I looked for someone who could build a wall, who could stand in the places where the walls have crumbled and defend the land when my anger is about to destroy it, but I could find no one." (Ezekiel 22:30)

- Intercession, though a manner of prayer, differs from ordinary praying. While prayer is a form of communicating, making a request, and supplicating. Intercession is standing in gap on behalf of others.

- It involves much labor, wrestling, and travailing. Because there is contention over the souls of men, the Bible says we have been delivered from the kingdom of darkness. (Colossians 1:13) Therefore there are many struggles to get men out and ensure they are not snatched back. A watchman will, therefore, need to pray through much more in prayer.

- Intercession is level of prayer above "Me, mine and I" requests. (Colossians 4:12. Galatians 4:19; Colossians 1:3; 9; 29; Isaiah 66:9)

- Intercession involves laboring and struggling to breakthrough in prayer. It is praying through and not about issues. Labor is translated from the word "KOPIAO," meaning to toil, to become weary. The word struggling is translated from the word "AGONIZOMAI." This is a Hebrew meaning to agonize, to fight, or to contend against.

According to Alice Smith in her book Beyond the Veil, "Intercession can literally order or change the course of a nation, a city, a family, or a church. Intercession is neither "emotional hype," rituals, prayer lists, nor obligations. It is a Spirit-led privilege. Magnificent and wonderful revelations have come because of prayer and intercession. These revelations result from intimate fellowship with the Lord

Call to Intercession

"And He saw that there was no man and wondered that there was no intercessor [no one to intervene on behalf of truth and right]; therefore, His own arm brought Him victory, and His own righteousness [having the Spirit without measure] sustained Him." (Isaiah 59:16 Ezekiel 22:30)

Examples of Intercessors in the bible are Abraham, Moses, Nehemiah, and Daniel (Genesis 18:16-33; Exodus 32;34; Daniel 9)

Promptings

It can come as a burden placed on your heart, just like the one Isaiah had when he had his life-changing encounter with God in the chapter of Isaiah. *"I heard the voice of the Lord, saying, whom shall I send? And who will go for us? Then said I, here am I; send me. And He said, Go and tell this people, Hear and hear continually, but understand not; and see and see continually, but do not apprehend with your mind."* (Isaiah 6:8-9)

Like when God introduced the subject of Sodom and Gomorrah to Abraham and negotiated with God on their behalf. (Genesis 18)

- A visual through picture flashes of a person or place with further instructions.

- Dream. (Acts 2: 17-18)

- A nudge in the spirit.

- A flash of a name or picture. Acts 9:10-14

- The sense of urgency.

- Burdens to pray for something else from your prayer list, as you continue in prayer; this may be, to intercept the plans of the enemy and to impose the will of God as revealed at the moment.

In one of the prayer ministries I led, we used to run a program called Prayer Summit at the end of the month. At the Summit we learned and prayed, and in the meetings, sudden burdens have been placed on individuals for urgent intervention which often diverts our attention but have prevented deaths by accidents or other incidents; often to the glory of God and to the shame of the devil.

As much as prayer lists or pre-prepared prayer points are good, be sensitive to the prompting of the Holy Spirit and instantly obey His instructions.

What Should Be Your Response?

- Rise up to the task. It is an act of obedience and agreement to enter a partnership with God in changing the course of a thing.

- Pray until there is a change or release; remember it is praying through and not about.

- Plead for mercy.

- Anticipate victory.

MARK OF AN INTERCESSOR:

- Possessing determination and purposefulness

- Motivated by the goal of victory

- Steadfast

- Unwavering

- Tenacious

- Firm

- Definite

- Persevering

- Passionate about delivering a successful outcome

- Ability to see things through

- Not giving up

An Intercessor Will Therefore:

- Pray longer than an average person

- Pray more times

- Make prayer a priority

- Be devoted to prayer activities

- Have burden for the things of God

- Be sensitive to issues and events around him/her. The spiritual watchman must be able to discern the spiritual battle in the heavenlies. They must also be able to discern the battle in the world, the city, the church, and in people seeing the past, present, and future. The watchman can then project this vision to the real world, praying the Kingdom and God's vision into existence in the world here. The prayer becomes a strategic prayer like the prayer of Daniel in Daniel 10

Intercession becomes a lifestyle for the intercessor and not a temporary chore. According to Dr. Terry Teykl, "True intercession is not just something you engage in one hour in a week; it's a way of life. It is motivated by a heart that can look past unlovable exteriors to see people as God intended them to be, and then pray that picture into existence when everyone else has given up."

MANY KINDS OF INTERCESSORS:

Different intercessors exist according to sphere and focus of influence. From my experience and observation with my team; some just like to pray for the church or the leadership, and when asked, the same person to pray for the nation, but they just cannot function as would have been expected.

IDENTIFYING INTERCESSORS

- WARFARE INTERCESSORS: These intercessors are more involved in spiritual warfare, either in individual life or for the corporate body. They bring to life 2 Corinthian 10:4 against the battles of Ephesians 6:12. Any Watchman who operates in this dimension of intercession must be able to work in the revelatory gifts. To be committed to fighting warfare, please be committed to God more and more. "The deep calleth unto the deep." (Psalms 42:7)

- PERSONAL INTERCESSORS: These Watchmen are moved to pray for personal needs of individuals under their watch. The needs could bother on spiritual, physical, or material. They usually adopt a people to pray for until there is a release, either due to death or termination on God's instruction. These are people that want to pray for personal needs of individuals when praying for corporate spiritual revival or national prayer. Their drive is fueled by the spiritual gift of mercy.

- CRISIS INTERCESSORS: These intercessors sense impending danger and alert others, and prayer is mobilized with immediate urgency. It works by the revelatory gift.

- FINANCIAL INTERCESSORS: They pray for the supply of resources of the church or projects. It is enhanced by the gift of faith. Believe that whatever project that the church embarks will succeed and God will always raise up his people that will sponsor the project. Therefore, prayers must continue so that people's heart will be touched to give and that the devil would not attack their finances they may have in abundance to give to the work of God.

- STRUCTURED INTERCESSORS: They prayed through prayer list. Structural intercessors have a list of prayers they pray with, and they adhere to the list as strictly as possible.

- GLOBAL INTERCESSORS: These are called to nations. They pray with passion for happenings all over the world. They stand in gap as the spirit gives them burdens. I remember the days of Iraq and Iran wars, and when we gathered to pray for service, some brethren must pray for Iraq and Iraq regardless. They pray for people and groups alongside.

- WORSHIP INTERCESSORS: These intercessors sing their prayer. Through worship, they communicate with God, and from there they might even sing in the spirit. It is also such a wonderful experience for such intercessors.

- GOVERNMENT INTERCESSORS: They pray for a different level of government.

- EVANGELISTIC INTERCESSORS: They pray for the salvation of souls. They pray for evangelistic outreaches and people involved in evangelism and crusades.

- SERVICE INTERCESSORS: They pray over service and on-going programs of the church. Engage in prayers before, during, and after service.

- LEADERSHIP INTERCESSORS: These Watchmen intercessors have callings to stand in gap for the leadership either spiritual or secular. Even though we have been instructed by Paul in 1 Timothy 2:1-4 to pray for all leaders, some people do it more earnestly, and most times God gives them a particular leader, and they don't stop until the person dies, or God decides to re-assign them.

The essence of this identification is to know who you are and improve on it. Room for change depends on the Holy Spirit. There can be a mixture of these traits in an individual. For instance, a watchman over a church will do warfare, do personal prayers, and will sometimes sense danger and mobilize others to pray, especially if he /she is a leader.

Another essential reason for the identification is to know how to work together in a team. Everybody does not have the same calling, burden, or passion, but all should be able to work together for a common goal, that the body of Christ is edified.

REFLECTIONS

- What potentials have you observed in you that can help you to serve effectively?

- What strategies have you used before to develop your potentials?

- Did you gain any new knowledge?

- What spiritual gifts do you have?

- Do you have any special burden to pray for?

CHAPTER 3

THE PURPOSE OF THE WATCHMAN

"Until purpose is discovered, existence has no meaning, for purpose is the source of fulfillment." - Myles Munroe

SCRIPTURE:

"I've posted WATCHMEN on your walls, Jerusalem. Day and night, they keep at it, praying, calling out, and reminding God to remember. They are to give him no peace until he does what he said, until he makes Jerusalem famous as the City of Praise." (Isaiah 62:6-7)

Though as believers we are all instructed to pray, (Luke 18:1) and sometimes God can prompt someone to stand in gap for a people or a purpose at any time and anywhere, but the call of a WATCHMAN is for an assigned period of time, over a place, a people, or purpose. The time could be short or long or ongoing. It is specific. It has a duration and place to it. It is more than prayer and intercession, but it engages both the instruments of prayer and intercession in its operation.

TO WHERE ARE YOU ASSIGNED?

This would be referring to the place of your watch. I would describe it as your sphere of influence. It could be geographical, physical, or spiritual. It could be a place or people or purpose or combination of it. You may have to be physically present or not. You may be assigned a remote territory where you cannot be physically connected to. Over the times people have been assigned over individuals who they have no affinity to, but names were given to them by God.

Watchmen are also assigned over local assembly; church in that regards, such ones will be responsible for the people, the purpose, and the place of the church. Since the church is not an isolated entity, that would then include the environment of the church, that is, the city, the state and the nations . Anything that affects these other entities will probably have a spiral effect upon the church itself . (John 17:17; Acts 2:47) You are expected to do your assignment with singleness of mind. (Romans 12:8; Ephesians 6:5)

Your faithfulness in little can cause enlargement (Luke 12:42-47)

Knowing your place helps in channeling your focus and energy, with this, could avoid meandering. You cannot be vagabond and be a successful watchman being here and there. And it does not make you paranoid as not to engage in other good works as needful or pray for other things.

Anna, the bible recorded was focused, with singleness of mind and motive, she was in the temple, praying and fasting for eighty–four years over one purpose, the coming of the Messiah. (Luke 2:36-37)

WHAT YOU ARE CALLED TO WATCH OUT FOR?

"Jesus went with them to a place called Gethsemane, and He told His disciples, sit down here while I go over yonder and pray. And taking with Him Peter and the two sons of Zebedee, He began to show grief and distress of mind and was deeply depressed. Then He said to them, my soul is very sad and deeply grieved, so that I am almost dying of sorrow. Stay here and keep awake and keep watch with Me. And going a little farther, He threw Himself upon the ground on His face and prayed saying, My Father, if it is possible, let this cup pass away from Me; nevertheless, not what I will [not what I desire], but as You will and desire. And He came to the disciples and found them sleeping, and He said to Peter, What! Are you so utterly unable to stay awake and keep watch with Me

for one hour? All of you must keep awake (give strict attention, be cautious and active) and watch and pray, that you may not come into temptation. The spirit indeed is willing, but the flesh is weak." (Matthew 26:36-41)

- Watching out for the enemy and withstand him on behalf of the body of Christ and more so, your subject of the watch. (1 Peter 5:8)

- Watching out for the wiles and intentions of Satan, to keep him from getting the advantage over the church. (2 Corinthians 2:11)

- Watching out for the temptation to prevent its infiltration. (Matthew 26:41)

For instance, the promise of God to Peter and the future church is that *"I will build my church, and the gates of Hades shall not prevail against it."* (Matthew 16:18)

We learned from the account in Act chapter twelve how the church was passive, until the arrest of Peter, it took that arrest to wake the church from slumbering and arising to pray, to stop the attack of the enemy.

"About that time Herod, the king, stretched forth his hands to afflict and oppress and torment some who belonged to the church (assembly) and he killed James the brother of John with a sword; and when he saw it was pleasing to the Jews, he proceeded further and arrested Peter also. This was during the days of Unleavened Bread [the Passover week]. And when he had seized [Peter], he put him in prison and delivered him to four squads of soldiers of four each to guard him, proposing after the

Passover to bring him forth to the people. So, Peter was kept in prison, but fervent prayer for him was persistently made to God by the church (assembly)" (Acts 12:1-5)

The fact that Jesus promised to build his church and the gates of Hades shall not prevail against it, does not prevent the enemy's attack on the first church, nor does it exclude us from fighting spiritual warfare. We still have that responsibility to fulfill.

The church that refuses to PRAY will become a PREY in the hand of the enemy. The nation in a shortage of WATCHMEN will be opened to the enemy's incursion and attacks and prone to problems.

The spiritual WATCHMAN is expected to detect the tactics of the enemy against the subject of his watch; protecting the church of God and the people of God. One tactic of the enemy is to hinder the work and men of God. (1 Thessalonians 2:18) Often we see Apostle Paul asking for prayers from the brethren. (1 Thessalonians 5:25)

- Watching out for anything that may want to hinder the word of God from spreading speedily. (2 Thessalonians 3:1-2)

- Watching the invasion of malicious and wicked men who lack faith and are ready to attack the purpose and the persons of God to hinder the manifestations of the glory of God. (2 Thessalonians 3:1-2)

Let us look at operating a WATCHMAN in the

situation between Elisha and the king of Israel versus the king of Syria in 2 Kings 6: 8-24.

- The king of Syria from his nation planned to launch an attack on Israel from a particular end and at a particular time. (8)

- Elisha as watchman foresaw this plan from his own end

- Sent a warning to the king of Israel. (9)

- The plan of the enemy was intercepted and foiled. (10)

- Elisha was sensitive in the spirit to know when danger was imminent.

"For thus has the Lord said to me: Go, set [yourself as] a watchman, let him declare what he sees. And when he sees a troop, horsemen in pairs, a troop of donkeys, and a troop of camels, he shall listen diligently, very diligently. And [the watchman] cried like a lion, O Lord, I stand continually on the watchtower in the daytime, and I am set in my station every night." (Isaiah 21:6-8)

- The watchmen watching over the city are expected to watch out for the ungodly messengers and the enemies. (2 Samuel 18:27)

- Watching out and keeping off Wolves. (Ezekiel 22:27; Zechariah 11:5; Acts 20:29)

- Watching out for fake prophets and their work.

(Matthew 7:15; Jeremiah 23:16)

- Watching out for Pollution through heresies and wrong doctrines. (2 Peter 2:1-2)

- To watch out for anything that endangers the vision or mission of the church.

- To watch out for anything that may want to divert or delay the manifestation of the promise

    It should be noted that:

- You are called to stand in gap not to stand against.

- You are called to be a defender and not an attacker.

- You are an advocate and not an adversary

- You are support, backup and not forefront ministry, but you can change the course of action behind the scenes.

For instance, if your area of jurisdiction is a local church you cannot join people to criticize your leaders regardless of their weaknesses. I once witnessed a church where the prayer leader was always attacking the leadership of the church, that they were supposed to be watching over. Those kinds will never move up from being just prayer leaders. It was so bad, it was like two churches within a church, the main church and the church of prayer warriors'. The prayer warriors hardly go to other functions of the church except for their meetings. That is not an attribute of a good watchman.

Our role is to stand behind the scenes for others in good times, for sustenance, and protection and the bad times, for restoration and refreshment; all to make sure the vision comes to pass. We can sense the disappointment of Apostle Paul when there was nobody to stand for him. (2 Timothy 4:18)

As a WATCHMAN you will need to always be sensitive to pick heavenly signals and notifications from the Holy Spirit of impending dangers from the enemy. Carelessness in watching will make the WATCHMAN miss the timely and godly warning and make the subject of watch prone to the enemy's attack.

- Jesus warned the disciple against the consequence of carelessness in watching for impending danger. (Mark 14:34-38)

- Watchful of the opportune time for the manifestation of God's promise and fulfillment of predictions. (Daniel 9:1-2; Luke 21:36)

- Watching out for the invasion of thieves. The watchman in the Old Testament often interchangeably described as guards protected the vineyards from thieves and animals and the marauders. (2 Kings 11:18; John 10:10)

- Pastors need to have trusted watchmen with strong manifestations of the gift of discerning of spirits whom they can listen to against pollutions, contamination, and infiltration. PASTORS,

PLEASE LISTEN TO YOUR WATCHMEN! THERE IS NO POINT HAVING A LEAD WATCHMAN YOU CANNOT TRUST. (Acts 20:28-31; Revelation:2)

TO WHOM HAVE YOU BEEN CALLED

The people, whom you are to serve, remember your service is for someone, over some other people. You are basically a steward of one over others.

When God calls a WATCHMAN, He also gives instruction on which people, God can raise a WATCHMAN over a family, over a nationality, and Ezekiel was appointed over the house of Israel while Jeremiah was appointed over the nations.

The earliest recollection of a physical WATCHMAN is in my childhood. In my house in those days, we used to have men manning the gatehouse, called the 'watch nights', even though some worked on afternoon shift they were called 'the watch nights'. Our watch nights stayed outside the main building in a small house armed with a Dane gun and whistles.

Basically, they stay outside awake while everybody else stays inside sleeping comfortably. A 'watch night' outside is enough to scare people away until the robbers in my home country became very daring.

You are not by yourself for yourself but for others, and you must be able to know how to provide needful service to them. But the thing about the spiritual

WATCHMAN compared to the physical watchman is that even you may know your people, but they may not know you. Anna and Simeon did not broadcast to the whole world they were praying for the coming of the Messiah. God may want you to be discreet or open about your service.

"And the Lord said, who then is that faithful steward, the wise man whom his master will set over those in his <u>household</u> service to supply them their allowance of food at the appointed time?" (Luke 12:42)

"Before I formed you in the womb I knew [and] approved of you [as My chosen instrument], and before you were born I separated and set you apart, consecrating you; [and] I appointed you as a prophet to the <u>nations.</u>" (Jeremiah 1:5)

"You, son of man, I have made you a watchman <u>for the house of Israel</u>; therefore, hear the word at my mouth and give them warning from Me." (Ezekiel 33:7)

REFLECTIONS

- What or who do you have the burden to pray for most times? That could reflect to whom you have been called to.

CHAPTER 4
THE PROFESSIONAL ETHICS OF THE WATCHMAN

"Once you realize that you're in something that you've always wanted, and you don't want to lose it, you behave differently. And that means the integrity, the professionalism and knowing what is right from wrong and still making choices that you probably wouldn't have made." - Paul Anka

Due to the demand of the assignment, it would be of necessity to put ethics in place that would determine the hallmark of a person that desires to succeed as a WATCHMAN. This is to serve as a source of encouragement and motivation to those who are already in the race as a WATCHMAN and those who are yet to enter the race.

The possession of these attributes will preserve and protect you, as you continue in this journey, as a WATCHMAN. We must continue to build right on the foundation already laid not in our own way but God's way, that at the end of it all our work will pass the test of fire and our reward will not be lost. (1 Corinthians 3:9-15)

To operate at a higher level of a WATCHMAN for God is compared to an ordinary prayer(er), you will need to work with these ethics in mind, and it will not just help you, but also distinguish you from the rest of the pack.

WHY DO WE NEED THIS?

That one may run the race as to obtain the mark (1 Corinthians 9:24) that also may run according to the rules, not ours, but God's, to obtain the crown (2 Timothy 2:5)

- That one may aim at satisfying the one who has enlisted him/her as a WATCHMAN. (2 Timothy 2:5)

- That one may be well informed about the task before him (2 Timothy 2:2; Hosea 4:6)

- That one may be proficient, well fitted and thoroughly equipped for the assignment (1 Timothy 3:16-17)

- To bridge the gap between expectation and service, the gap between the WATCHMAN's actual standard of performance and the expectations of God and other stakeholders respectively; for instance, the leadership and the members of a local assembly.

- *That at the end we may boldly and convincingly say, "I have fought a good fight the good (worthy, honorable, and noble fight), I have finished the race, I have kept (firmly held) the faith.* (2 Timothy 4:7)

WHAT IS A HALLMARK?

- It is a distinguishing characteristic, trait or feature that set one besides others.

- It is the mark of excellence, a mark indicating the quality of excellence. It is what makes one's WATCHMAN calling or ministry effective and efficient. (James 5:16)

CASE STUDY

To help us further we shall slot in the story of David who had to fight through many odds and adversity for a period spanning almost over twenty years to become what he was ordained to become, and yet did not give up or quit fighting. Like David, a WATCHMAN, has to engage in battles for the glory of the LORD to be revealed over a place or people, though on a different terrain. While David fought physical battles, today our battles are fought in the spiritual realms and not on the field, but on the knees in the place of prayer.

Like someone said, "The great battles, the battles

that decide our destiny and destiny of generations yet unborn, are not fought on the public platforms, but in the lonely hours of the night and in moment of agony."__ Samuel Logan Brengle.

ATTRIBUTES TO POSSESS:

Knowledge

- Knowledge is described as the fact or condition of knowing that something with familiarity gained through experience or association. It is the fact or condition of being aware of something. As a WATCHMAN it is needful to know certain facts relating to the subject of WATCHING. If you are watching over a church, you must know things about that church.

- Knowledge is also defined as the sum of what is known: the body of truth, information, and principles acquired by mankind. As WATCHMEN, these are bodies of truth and principles that will help in pushing through in attaining the set goal, the lack of knowledge of those will make the task hard and discouraging and even destructive. (Hosea 4:6)

In this work we cannot just assume things or jump the gun; it will be safe to know. How do you get to know? It is by asking questions and by careful observations?

Now, let us look at David's confrontation with Goliath as a case study:

"Now the Philistines gathered their armies for battle and were assembled at Socoh, which belongs to Judah, and encamped between Socoh and Azekah in Ephes-dammim. Saul and the men of Israel were encamped in the Valley of Elah and drew up in battle array against the Philistines. And the Philistines stood on a mountain on one side, and Israel stood on a mountain on the other side, with the valley between them. And a champion went out of the camp of the Philistines named Goliath of Gath, whose height was six cubits and a span [almost ten feet].

And he had a bronze helmet on his head and wore a coat of mail, and the coat weighed 5,000 shekels of bronze. He had bronze shin armor on his legs and a bronze javelin across his shoulders. And the shaft of his spear was like a weaver's beam; his spear's head weighed 600 shekels of iron. And a shield-bearer went before him. Goliath stood and shouted to the ranks of Israel, why have you come out to draw up for battle? Am I not a Philistine, and are you not servants of Saul? Choose a man for yourselves and let him come down to me. If he can fight with me and kill me, then we will be your servants; but if I prevail against him and kill him, then you shall be our servants and serve us. And the Philistine said, I defy the ranks of Israel this day; give me a man, that we may fight together. When Saul and all Israel heard those words of the Philistine, they were dismayed and greatly afraid. David was the son of an Ephrathite of Bethlehem in Judah named Jesse, who had eight sons. [Jesse] in the days of Saul was old, advanced in years. [His] three eldest sons had followed Saul into battle. Their names were Eliab the firstborn;

next, Abinadab; and third, Shammah. David was the youngest. The three eldest followed Saul, But David went back and forth from Saul to feed his father's sheep at Bethlehem. The Philistine came out morning and evening, presenting himself for forty days. And Jesse said to David his son, take for your brothers an ephah of this parched grain and these ten loaves and carry them quickly to your brothers at the camp. Also take these ten cheeses to the commander of their thousand. See how your brothers fare and bring some token from them. Now Saul and the brothers and all the men of Israel were in the Valley of Elah, fighting with the Philistines. So, David rose up early next morning, left the sheep with a keeper, took the provisions, and went, as Jesse had commanded him. And he came to the encampment as the host going forth to the battleground shouted the battle cry. And Israel and the Philistines put the battle in array, army against army. David left his packages in the care of the baggage keeper and ran into the ranks and came and greeted his brothers. As they talked, behold, Goliath, the champion, the Philistine of Gath, came forth from the Philistine ranks and spoke the same words as before, and David heard him. And all the men of Israel, when they saw the man, fled from him, terrified. And the Israelites said, have you seen this man who has come out? Surely, he has come out to defy Israel; and the man who kills him the king will enrich with great riches and will give him his daughter and make his father's house free [from taxes and service] in Israel. And David said to the men standing by him, what shall be done for the man who kills this Philistine and takes away the reproach from Israel? For who is this uncircumcised Philistine that he should defy the armies of the living God? And the [men] told him, thus shall it *be done for the man who kills him. Now Eliab his eldest brother heard what he said to the men; and Eliab's anger was kindled against David and he said, why did you come here? With whom have you left those few sheep in the wilderness? I know your presumption and evilness of heart; for you came down that you might see the battle. And David said, what have I done now? Was it not a harmless question?*

And David turned away from Eliab to another and he asked the same question, and again the men gave him the same answer. When David's words were heard, they were repeated to Saul, and he sent for him. David said to Saul, let no man's heart fail because of this Philistine; your servant will go out and fight with him.

And Saul said to David, you are not able to go to fight against this Philistine. You are only an adolescent, and he has been a warrior from his youth. And David said to Saul, your servant kept his father's sheep. And when there came a lion or again a bear and took a lamb out of the flock, I went out after it and smote it and delivered the lamb out of its mouth; and when it arose against me, I caught it by its beard and smote it and killed it. Your servant killed both the lion and the bear; and this uncircumcised Philistine shall be like one of them, for he has defied the armies of the living God! David said, The Lord Who delivered me out of the paw of the lion and out of the paw of the bear, He will deliver me out of the hand of this Philistine. And Saul said to David, Go, and the Lord be with you!" (1 Samuel 17)

We saw David at the battlefield listening to the discussion and after that making inquiries. He did not just jump into the battle, he asked questions. In this work, there are things to know. You cannot assume things. The things you seek to know about this assignment constitutes the knowledge that will help you to make it as a WATCHMAN.

In your effort to watch, you must be observant. David could have just left the supplies and left the battlefield without his interference and missed a great deal to be used of God in the deliverance of Israel, but he looked, listened, and inquired. One responsibility of a WATCHMAN is to observe and look out. As a WATCHMAN you must be inquisitive. Another person who was observant and inquisitive was Moses. Had he ignored the burning bush, he would have missed out a great deal on his calling as a deliverer he meant to be. When he stopped to ponder over what he saw, he got more information on what was expected of him from God. (Exodus 3:1-4) When you see strange things make inquiries physically and spiritually.

The question is what do you make out of the news you listen to? What are the things you observe when you are near your church, what about the people? When the pastor preaches, can you discern the burden on his heart to take on in the place of prayer? Whatever you see or hear may be a pointer to something you need to work on in the place of prayer.

Knowledge also prepares and motivates you for the

job. While it is good to be zealous to do the job, it must be accompanied by knowledge. (Romans 10:2)

Knowledge comes from Previous Experience, education, [formal and informal] training, familiarity, vision blueprints map, history, and information gathered from others.

WHAT DO YOU NEED TO KNOW?

- You need to know your God, like David. (2 Timothy 1:12; Daniel 11:32)

- You need to know who and what you are fighting against. (Ephesians 6:12)

- You need to know your weapons of warfare. (2 Corinthians 10:3-4)

- You need to know how and when to engage the weapons. (1 Chronicles 12:32)

- You are called and appointed on a special assignment not for you, but for others. You are a steward to another. (1 Samuel 16:1; Jeremiah 1:5; 1 Timothy 1:12) Therefore your service must be selfless, Christ-centered and not self-centered.

- You are a new creation. (2 Corinthians. 5:17-21) Your place is in heavenly places as an expression of His grace. (Ephesians 2:6]

- You are a bride and helpmate. (Genesis 2:18) you are not independent, you are to complement Him in partnership with the extension of the kingdom. (Matthew. 6: 9-10, 33) You are a fellow workman, joint promoter, and laborer with God and He, being the senior partner. Always have it in mind except the Lord keeps the city, the watchman wakes but in vain. (Psalm 127:1b)

- You are not appointed because you are better than anybody else. It is a privilege that should not be abused. (Ephesians 2:8-9)

- You are representing others in the court of heaven. An example is Abraham negotiating with God on behalf of the righteous in Sodom and Gomorrah. (Genesis 18:23-32) Moses also stood in gap for the Israelites that God would not destroy on their coming out of Egypt. (Exodus 32:11-12) Jesus, our ultimate model, also prayed for His disciples, petitioning the court of heaven to deliver them from the evil world. (John 17:9, 20)

- You are a priest. (Hebrew 7:11-28)

- To be all of the above, the first qualification is that you must be born again. You must be on the side of God translated and rescued from the kingdom of darkness. (Colossians 1:13) For a kingdom cannot be divided against itself and still stand. (Matthew 12:25)

HOW TO WORK THE WORK

Like it was said earlier you cannot assume things and jump the gun, you have to know what to do. When Moses was called, he asked questions on how and with whom. These are not one-time questions. As you continue, you must constantly seek God's counsel and divine strategy for each cause. Constantly David asks questions. That is why intimacy with God, Jesus, and the Holy Spirit is unavoidable. In the book of 1 Samuel 30 after the Amalekites had attacked Ziklag and took away their possessions and family, he did not just jump to fight, he made inquiries as what to do. (1 Samuel 30:7-10)

Not forgetting the exploits that led to the fall of Jericho in Joshua chapter six. Gideon and his army in Judges in chapter seven.

"NOW MOSES kept the flock of Jethro his father-in-law, the priest of Midian; and he led the flock to the back or west side of the wilderness and came to Horeb or Sinai, the mountain of God. The Angel of the Lord appeared to him in a flame of fire out of the midst of a bush; and he looked, and behold, the bush burned with fire, yet was not consumed. And Moses said, I will now turn aside and see this great sight, why the bush is not burned. And when the Lord saw that he turned aside to see, God called to him out of the midst of the bush and said, Moses, Moses! And he said, here am I. God said, do not come near; put your shoes off your feet, for the place on which you stand is holy ground. Also, He said, I am

the God of your father, the God of Abraham, the God of Isaac, and the God of Jacob. And Moses hid his face, for he was afraid to look at God. And the Lord said, I have surely seen the affliction of My people who are in Egypt and have heard their cry because of their taskmasters and oppressors; for I know their sorrows and sufferings and trials. And I have come down to deliver them out of the hand and power of the Egyptians and to bring them up out of that land to a land good and large, a land flowing with milk and honey [a land of plenty] --to the place of the Canaanite, the Hittite, the Amorite, the Perizzite, the Hivite, and the Jebusite.

Now behold, the cry of the Israelites has come to Me, and I have also seen how the Egyptians oppress them. Come now therefore, and I will send you to Pharaoh, that you may bring forth My people, the Israelites, out of Egypt. And Moses said to God, who am I, that I should go to Pharaoh and bring the Israelites out of Egypt? God said, I will surely be with you; and this shall be the sign to you that I have sent you: when you have brought the people out of Egypt, you shall serve God on this mountain [Horeb, or Sinai]. And Moses said to God, Behold, when I come to the Israelites and say to them, The God of your fathers has sent me to you, and they say to me, what is His name? What shall I say to them?

And God said to Moses, I AM WHO I AM and WHAT I AM, and I WILL BE WHAT I WILL BE; and He said, you shall say this to the Israelites: I AM has sent me to you! God said also to Moses, this shall you say to the Israelites: The Lord, the God of your fathers, of Abraham, *of Isaac, and of Jacob, has sent me to you! This is My name forever, and by this name I am to be remembered to all generations.*

Go, gather the elders of Israel together [the mature teachers and tribal leaders], and say to them, The Lord God of your fathers, the God of Abraham, of Isaac, and of Jacob, appeared to me, saying, I have surely visited you and seen that which is done to you in Egypt; And I have declared that I will bring you up out of the affliction of Egypt to the land of the Canaanite, the Hittite, the Amorite, the Perizzite, the Hivite, and the Jebusite, to a land flowing with milk and honey.

And [the elders] shall believe and obey your voice; and you shall go, you and the elders of Israel, to the king of Egypt and you shall say to him, The Lord, the God of the Hebrews, has met with us; and now let us go, we beseech you, three days' journey into the wilderness, that we may sacrifice to the Lord our God. And I know that the king of Egypt will not let you go [unless forced to do so], no, not by a mighty hand. So, I will stretch out My hand and smite Egypt with all My wonders which I will do in it; and after that he will let you go. And I will give this people favor and respect in the sight of the Egyptians; and it shall be that when you go, you shall not go empty-handed. But every woman shall [insistently] solicit of her neighbor and of her that may be residing at her house jewels and articles of silver and gold, and garments, which you shall put on your sons and daughters; and you shall strip the Egyptians [of belongings due to you]."
(Exodus 3)

- In carrying out this assignment, you have to develop strategies aligning with the will of God. You cannot work any way you want, but how God wants it to be done.

- You must know people to work with, not everybody can fit into the role of a WATCHMAN, I'm not trying to put anyone down; not everyone will have that staying power and that is why it is not an office you apply for, it is a Divine appointment. God sought for intercessors. (Ezekiel 22:30) but appointed WATCHMEN. (Isaiah 62:6-7)

When God told me, I have appointed you as a watchman over my church, He also said I have raised others too, but I ran ahead of Him to make a general call, but most people that joined initially fell off, and I prayed, and He then revealed the real people, and I approached them. On my last assignment, I tried to push people, until one day I heard the voice of the Holy Spirit while driving, "You cannot make people to become what I have not made them to be." If you must be a leader of a team, you then must be careful in calling in people; it is of God to do the calling, yours is to identify. God appointed Moses when it was time to have somebody else it was God that instructed Moses to ordain Joshua. (Deuteronomy 31:14-15) For David, he was tendering sheep when God sent Samuel to go ordain him. (1 Samuel 16:1) and Elisha was plowing Oxen when Elijah ordained him as his successor on God's instruction. (1 Kings 19:19 -21)

- From all indication, the WATCHMEN for a nation may just be a person, after all, John Knox, we heard prayed over Scotland. Jeremiah was appointed at a time over the nations. (Jeremiah 1:5) So, for a church of a thousand, the WATCHMEN, may not be more than twenty-five.

- Your choice is not because you are better than anybody else, but that because you are appointed for this purpose, God has graced and equipped you for it.

- It should also be noted that the initiative does not come from you, but from God, so you have to wait on him for instructions.

- You must be very sensitive in the spirit and also observe unusual happenings and sights.

- You have to develop a spiritual strategy to fit into your assignment and for adequate coverage. For instance, as a church team, you can institute a 24-hour watch divided into hours, and you have reliable people covering each hour, batons passing from hand to hand.

- If your watch is over a church develop a prayer strategy that works with the vision of the church, providing adequate coverage, that is why the team idea is good. After all, it is Watchmen and not a Watchman posted. (Isaiah 62:6-7)

- If you are watching over a church get to know the

vision of the church.

- If you are watching over a geographical territory, that you cannot be physically present for, obtain the map and history of the place to get to know them.

- You will need to know how to pray intelligently and to do this; the watchman must know of different kind of prayers and how to apply to each situation. [Ephesians 6:18]

WHO DO YOU REPORT TO?

- Work knowing that God is your employer and the recruiter. Therefore, the agenda you will follow will not be that of man but God's. God by Himself does the posting. He will set and appoint a person as a watchman over a family, city, nation, or a local assembly (Church) over time and for a purpose. He deploys and redeploys.

- The fear of human opinion disables; sufficient enough to say your employer is God. You are therefore accountable to Him.

- You, therefore, have to be kingdom conscious and focused. *"Let thy kingdom come and let thy will be done"* will be your highest priority rather than self-building or people pleasing.

- You need to have the Knowledge of God. (Daniel 11:32) Not just knowing about Him but knowing him intimately. That is the only way to work and walk in his ways to please Him. He showed Moses His ways, he who knows His ways can perform His acts. (Psalm 103:7)

- Know to whom you are responsible to. While respecting the earthly supervisors in whatever office they occupy over you, it is also of importance to know the ultimate boss over you all. (Ephesians 6:8)

The knowledge of the above will help you:

- To stay off playing politics.

- Trusting in God to protects you from that. *"Everyone tries to get help from the leader, but only GOD will give us justice.* (Proverbs 29:26)

- Not to be scouting for position

- From being manipulative.

- To know your employer is your rewarder, not man.

WHAT AUTHORITY

- A watchman authority to act is derived from the term of his appointment or assignment, and it flows from the assignor who is God to the assignee. You are acting for God, representing him. Your authority is therefore informed by the term of your appointment. (Ezekiel 33:3 -7)

THE GAME PLAN OF THE ENEMY

- You should not be ignorant of the schemes and tactics of the adversary and his threat to the manifestation of the promise of God. You are to watch out for his attacks and encroachment. You can miss this if you are ignorant of his tactics and can also fall a victim of his tactics if you are careless. There was a time I invited a US Marine officer to come and teach us military intelligence for us to gain some understanding of warfare, and it helped my team. (Ephesians 6:11; 2 Corinthians 2:11)

WHAT WEAPONS

You will need to know the weapons of the enemy (Isaiah 54:17) and the weapons available to you for both offensive and defensive. (Isaiah 54:16)

As a WATCHMAN you will need to work with working knowledge of weapons available to work in your Watching.

- Fighting in the defense and protection of your watch will not be by any carnal method but by spiritual methods and with spiritual weapons. It will be of necessity to know and be acquainted with these weapons. Know, for any weapons of the enemy, God has a weapon to counter their effort (Isaiah 59:19)

- Whenever God has a plan for a people or a

place the enemy always has a counter plan. For instance, in Zechariah 1: 16-21, immediately God announced His plan for the restoration and the rebuilding of Jerusalem we saw the enemy advancing with his own weapons of destruction to scatter, but it was intercepted by God's own weapon to build. Some weapons are meant for the pulling down and some for the planting. You must know what, how, and when to use.

- David, our person, was knowledgeable about his weapon. He dares not use an untested weapon. (1 Samuel 17:39-40, 45, 49) Practice they say makes perfect. Perfection makes you acquainted with your weapon and results in making the use of the weapon effective. (1 Corinthians 12:1)

- Must not be ignorant of spiritual gifts and weapons needful in the discharge of his/her duty. He must know and be equipped with such. (1 Corinthian 12. Ephesians 6: 11-18; Romans 12: 6 -11)

SOURCE OF THE WATCHMAN'S KNOWLEDGE

- The scripture. Knowledge of the word is very important.

- The institutional God's given written vision (Habakkuk 3:1-3; Daniel 9:2)

- Experts. (books, seminars, conferences, mentoring)

- Personal experiences. (1 Samuel 17: 32-37)

UNDERSTANDING

"Through wisdom a house is built, and by understanding it is established;" (Proverb. 24:3)

You have discovered that you are a WATCHMAN and you know of all that is enumerated above, but that is not where it stops It is not enough to know, it is better to understand. So, it would be better to grasp the meaning on your call and responsibility as a WATCHMAN

- Your ability to perceive and explain the meaning or nature of your purpose and responsibility.

- You must be able to interpret your role.

- You must understand the subject of your watch. The circumstances and situation around them.

- You need insight and the grace to comprehend situations.

"Of the sons of Issachar who had understanding of the times, to know what Israel ought to do, their chiefs were two hundred; and all their brethren were at their command." (1 Chronicles 12:32)

For a watchman to be distinguished,

there must be corresponding understanding of

- TIMING: You must be sensitive to divine timing as related to a vision. Ignorance of the timing will cause loss of opportunity. This might be the reason why the Israelites had to stay thirty years longer in Egypt than was planned by God. God told Abraham in Genesis 15 that his descendants will stay in a strange land for 400 years after which they shall come out, but they had to do extra 30 years because most likely nobody knew the understood the time as call on God earlier. *"In the first year of his reign, I, Daniel, understood from the books the number of years which, according to the word of the Lord to Jeremiah the prophet, must pass by before the desolations [which had been] pronounced on Jerusalem should end; and it was seventy years.*"(Daniel 9:2) Daniel was referring to the prophecy earlier given by prophet Jeremiah in Jeremiah 10:10-14

- It is not enough to receive a message and vision, understand them because misunderstanding can bring destruction not just on yourself, but also on the very thing you are watching over. You must diligently study and meditate on what you know, to gain understanding. *"Be that student that diligently studies to show yourself approved unto God, a worker who needs to be ashamed, rightly dividing the word of truth."* (2 Timothy 2:15)

- Understand that revelation may have been received, but there is appointed a time for the manifestation. (Habakkuk 2:2; Daniel 10:1) This will help you to work and wait patiently.

The period between the promise and the fulfillment is the period you have to be involved calling on God until there is a manifestation. If you do not understand this time, you will become agitated and disturb the completion of a process. As you continue in this process is the peace of God that keeps you in check. (Isaiah 26:3)

- You need to understand the assignment; That is, your job description. The sons of Issachar did not just understand the times, but they knew what Israel ought to do. (1 Chronicles 12:32)

- When you understand your assignment, you will need no one to pamper you before you stand by your command. (1 Chronicles 12:32)

- You must understand the expectation of God from you.

- You must understand the spiritual and physical environment to align with timing and purpose of God.

- The battle you have been enlisted to fight in.

- The weapons are available to him/her to fight in the battle. (1 Samuel 17:38-39) One must be familiar with the weapons available at his/her disposal and how and when to use each. David is an example of watchman warrior that knew how to use his weapons. Understanding grants, you're the mastery of the weapon. Of the David troop, the Zebulun were described as experts in a war with all weapons of warfare. (1 Chronicles 12:33)

- Having an understanding of your weapons does not just make you an expert in warfare but makes you prepared for battles and warfare.

"So, Saul clothed David with his armor, and he put a bronze helmet on his head; he also clothed him with a coat of mail. [39] David fastened his sword to his armor and tried to walk, for he had not tested them. And David said to Saul, "I cannot walk with these, for I have not tested them." So, David took them off." (1 Samuel 17:38-39)

- David refused to use the armor given to him by Saul because he did not know nor understood the weapon. He preferred to use what he understood and prevail against the enemy.

- It is better to avoid brandishing weapons you don't understand before the enemy, it is an open door for destruction.

An example of a weapon is the sword of truth, which is the word of God. That a word is in the bible does not mean it may be appropriate for a situation.

I see many people quoting words even when it is unnecessary, especially when other people are around just to show off. David would have been destroyed had he accepted to use Saul's weapon, he did not understand and was unfamiliar with it, but to create an impression; the devil would have outsmarted him.

Stick to the stone you know how to use and in the closet, behind the closed doors practice and perfect the use of other weapons. (1 Samuel 17:49)

- Understanding helps you to discern between the good and the evil. (1 king 3:9)

How do you gain understanding?

- It is Spirit. (Exodus 31:3; Isaiah 11:2)

- The Spirit gives understanding. (Job 32:8; Proverbs 2:6)

- The source is God. It comes by meditating on God's Word

- You have to deliberately seek for it, it is not superficial and cannot not be gotten on the surface. (Proverbs 15:4)

Why do you need to have understanding?

- Understanding makes you better than others. It distinguishes you.

- Understanding grants your mastery over matters. (Psalm.119:99;1 Samuel 16:16-21)

- Understanding of your role, your authority, your enemy and the weapons at your disposal protects you from becoming a casualty of war. (1 Samuel 17: 38-40)

- Understanding protects you from spiritual and physical death. (Proverbs 2:11; 21:16)

- Understanding of what you do will grant you access to unsolicited promotion. Daniel had understanding of times and was able to interpret the will and purpose of God for a nation and this earned promotion often. (Daniel 5:12,14)

- Understanding will preserve you from going weary.

- Understanding your commission will keep you from contamination and pollution. (Daniel 11:35)

- Understanding your assignment will make you outstanding.

WISDOM

"In Him all the treasures of [divine] wisdom (comprehensive insight into the ways and purposes of God) and [all the riches of spiritual] knowledge and enlightenment are stored up and lie hidden." (Colossians 2:3)

You must not just have knowledge and understanding but also must know how to apply what you know. It is propelled by the quality of experience you have acquired. Possession of wisdom makes you make sound judgment and action in regards to the knowledge you possess.

Wisdom is the application of acquired knowledge; it is not enough to have knowledge but know how to use it. A lot of wisdom is required in dealing with leaders, colleagues, and other people.

- It is needful in handling situations and people vertically or horizontal. "By wisdom you build your practice just like any other professional practice." (Proverbs 24:3 -4)

- It is required in the delivery of messages to the recipient

- Wisdom like knowledge is acquired in the same way

To make a mark in this call, you must develop the ability to make wise decisions and judgments based on experience and knowledge. You must be able to perceive situations.

It is having insight into the true nature of circumstance. Having this wisdom will make you not judge matter on the surface appearance, but help you to seek in-depth knowledge, or else you will be dealing with symptoms rather than the root cause of issues. You must be able to have a wide scope on issues.

Wisdom, as applied here, has the wide knowledge to decide and solve complex issues. It also helps us to know how to relate with others, be its superior or subordinates.

For instance, wisdom will help you know if a battle is

just a diversionary plan of the enemy.

The watchman that wants to make a success of his vocation must be able to use his/her discretion as to know:

- What kind of weapons to use. (1 Samuel 17:38-40; 45-47)

- When to apply certain principles and what kind of prayer to pray at a given time.

- Where to carry out his / her assignment as a watchman.

- How to present matters. A watchman must be able to present wisely and with discretion.

- Must be able to handle battle wisely. Some battles might arise that need a lot of wisdom to handle. Spiritual battles must be handled spiritually, a watchman will not go physically to fight or question an individual about something that is for the spirit realm.

- In dealing with others and issues. You may not be in leadership. Leaders are not the only ones that must be able to deal with other people and issues. As a watchman, you may face a challenge of having to deal with other people sometimes.

- Wisdom to keep things in order. (1 Chronicles 12:32-38)

Source of wisdom

- Number one source is God. (Exodus 31:3; Ezra 7:25; Proverbs 2:10)

- It is obtainable through the word. (Proverbs 3:13; Proverb 4:5)

- It can be gained through experience. It is wise to learn from your mistake. (Proverbs 3:13;1 Samuel 17:33-37)

- It is a spirit. (Exodus 34:9; Isaiah 11:2)

- It is transferable. (Deuteronomy 34:9)

- It is obtainable by asking for it. (James 1:5)

- Wisdom can be developed. (Luke 2:52)

- Wisdom also must be desperately and diligently pursued (Ecclesiastes 7:23-25)

- It distinguishes you. (Proverbs 3:13)

- Wisdom also protects you from destruction. (Proverbs 4:7)

- Wisdom makes you strong on the battlefield. (Ecclesiastes 7:19)

- It is needful in your assignment. (Acts 6:3)

- Waging war is needful. (Proverbs 21:22; 24:6; Ecclesiastes 9:14:18; Luke 14:31-32)

- Wisdom to count the cost. (Hosea 14:9)

ZEALOUSNESS

"If a man is called to be a street sweeper he should sweep the streets as Michelangelo painted, or Beethoven composed music or Shakespeare wrote poetry. He should sweep the streets so well that all the hosts of heaven and earth will pause and say, 'Here lived a great street sweeper who did his job so well." - Dr Martin Luther King Junior

SCRIPTURE

"David asked the men standing near him, what shall be done for the man who kills this Philistine and removes this disgrace from Israel? <u>Who is this uncircumcised Philistine that he should defy the armies of the living God.</u>" (1 Samuel 17:26)

For the assignment like that of the watchman that requires long time investment and probably lonesome, imagining everybody inside the comfort of their home and bed, and you have to stay awake watching, you would need a driving force. The driving force would be zeal, passion for what you do, it is sacrificial. (Joshua 24:15; 2 Samuel 24:3)

You can loudly hear David expressing his zeal for the things of God here:

"For zeal for your house has eaten me up, and the reproaches and insults of those who reproach and insult you have fallen upon me." (Psalms 69:9)

- You must believe in what you are doing, and believe in the one who has commissioned you, that He can do what He has promised to do, that will provoke the eagerness and ardent interest in pursuit of a mission to go all the way for Him. David said, *"The Lord who delivered me out of the paw of lion and the paw of the bear, He will deliver me out of the hand of the Philistine."* (1 Samuel 17:37)

- You must have and develop a keen enthusiasm and intense desire to see the will of God established over the entity or institution you have been assigned to watch over (Matthew 6:10) The ultimate goal in all situations is that God may be glorified.

- You cannot afford to be indifferent to things around you, especially when things are not working according to purpose; that is why one duty of a WATCHMAN is 'to observe', David observed something was not right, and he chose to make a difference. The Zeal for God, and the things of God make you stand out for God.

- There must be an eagerness to stand in watch. The king's business requires haste, you cannot afford to delay, and there must be readiness in you to go just as Isaiah did. (Isaiah 6:8)

- Zeal is propelled by the love of God and the people of God (Romans 10:2) In David we saw the demonstration of the zeal for the love of God when he declared "who is this uncircumcised Philistine that he should defy the army of the living God?" (1 Samuel 17:26b) So like Jesus, you must be zealous in loving righteousness and eager to promote the cause of righteousness, and you must also hate wickedness and be ready to fight against any prevailing wickedness against godly institutions and purpose.

- Zeal must be matched by knowledge, or there may be a casualty. (Romans 10:2) You must be enlightened according to correct and vital knowledge. Do not do things on your own without the leading and backing of the Holy Spirit and do not act with the grace you don't have. (Acts 19:11-16)

- The ministry of the WATCHMEN is a service unto God, and like any other service, you must be consumed with the zeal to serve. (Romans 12:11)

- Zeal/passion will be the motivating or the driving force that will make you pray and stand in gap for the Church, nations, and others without seeking any human's reward.

- A passionate person uses the information around them to bring about a change. [Ezra and Nehemiah] Zeal drives your action towards an issue. Watchmen are change agents.

We were admonished by Apostle Paul that, *"Whatever you do work at with all your heart, as working for the Lord, not for men."* (Colossians 3:23)

You should always have it in mind that your employer is God, and it is not in vain (Colossians 3:24) enjoined further, "Since you know that you will receive an inheritance from the Lord as a reward. It is the Lord Jesus Christ you are serving." Let the hope of reward motivate you or be a driving force for your zeal to watch. David asked, "What will be done for the man who kills this Philistine and remove this disgrace from Israel?" (1 Samuel 17:26)

• You must be passionate about what you do, if not find something you can be passionate about.

A watchman that is not passionate about praying for the kingdom business or cause relating to others cannot be a successful watchman period! You can see David in demonstrating his zeal when he said, *"Is there not a cause?"* (I Samuel 17:29) Nehemiah and Ezra were passion driven. (Nehemiah 13:15-28)

Remember you are fighting for a cause. What is that cause? That God may be glorified. You have to pray until a promise comes to pass and the devil is put to shame.

COMPASSIONATE/LOVE

"It is only love that can fit us for the work of intercession." Andrew Murray

SCRIPTURE

"And may the Lord make you increase and excel and overflow in love for one another and for all people, just as we also do for you." (1 Thessalonians 3:12)

- There should be empathy with the subject, be it a people or a cause. Identifying with the feelings, pains, and ultimate reward of the outcome of the prayer of intercession. It means putting yourself in the place of another. (Moses Exodus 32:9-14) Daniel in interceding for the nation of Israel identified himself with the people and the subject. (Daniel 9)

- You must be sensitive to your environments. You must be genuinely concerned about what concerns God, that is His purpose, and His people. An indifferent attitude will be a minus by Watchman that would want to excel in ministry.

- You cannot be judgmental. As a Watchman, you must operate from a compassionate angle and not be judgmental. (Hosea 6:6) You can learn from Abraham.(Genesis 18:20-33; Matthew 7:1-2)

- Not rejecting. You cannot afford to reject praying for certain people while accepting to do for others because of personal differences.

- Not ignorant. You cannot play ignorance, and that is why we have talked extensively about knowledge.

- Not excluding: You cannot play the exclusion game. You must cover all, don't add exclusion clause to your term of coverage.

- You must be compassionate regardless of any prejudice against you.

- Be able to pray for others regardless of treatment from them. No matter how people treat you as a watchman, you should be able to still pray and intercede for them. An example is [Moses versus Miriam and Aaron.] (Numbers 12)

- It emphasizes sacrifice by the watchman (Exodus 32:32; Esther 4:16; John 15:13)

- As a WATCHMAN on the way up, you must develop a sympathetic consciousness of others in distress tougher with a desire to alleviate it. David saw a nation in distress about to go into bondage and quickly rose to defend it. (1 Samuel 17) like Ezekiel, you will sometimes have to bear the iniquity and burden of others. (Ezekiel 4:4) You must, therefore, be willing to feel and bear the burdens of those you are watching over. (Hebrew 7:25; Luke 6:36)

FAITHFULNESS

"By faithfulness we are collected and wound up into unity within ourselves, whereas we had been scattered abroad in multiplicity." - St. Augustine

SCRIPTURE

"Moreover, it is [essentially] required of stewards that a man should be found faithful [proving himself worthy of trust]" (1 Corinthians 4:2)

It is to display some sense of responsibility or devotion to your assignment disregarding inconveniences.

- As a steward of another, you have to be faithful to your employer and your master, who is God and having an unwavering belief in Him whom you call on in prayer. You must believe in His will for you.

- You have to be faithful in the performance of your assignment.

- You must be faithful to the ministry and the meetings you are expected to participate in.

- You must be faithful to your church and the leadership

- Faithfulness makes you stand in your watchtower even when it is seemingly uncomfortable or inconvenient for you.

- You must firmly believe in what you are called to do and in whatever you are assigned to do; for like David asked, "is there not a cause?" Power and ability to answer prayers. Must believe in the course for which the prayer is being made.

- You must firmly believe in the one that has called you. The Hebrew trio were examples of people who knew and believe in the one who engaged them, and they were helped in their battle. (Daniel 3)

- You must believe in the cause you are upholding and fighting for. When you believe in a project, it makes your work easier, it's a kind of motivation. For instance, as a WATCHMAN over a church you must believe in the vision of the church and embrace the mission of the church and the leadership, failure to do this will cause struggles standing–in-gap for the church or any institution you are expected to watch over.

- Consistency is a key factor that must be put into consideration. It is not enough to do the right thing but to be consistent. You must be consistently loyal especially when you promise to engage in an assignment. You must be able to follow through, that is required in a person that will need to call on God until something happens. You must be consistent regardless of who is watching or not; regardless of recognition or appreciation. Consistency is required especially when answers to prayers seem delayed.

- Whenever you are given a project over time, be able to be counted on, that you will not fail. For instance, let's assume you have a 24-hour watch and you are to take a 1-hour slot for the next 40 days. Be trusted to discharge your duty as required with minimal to no supervision.

- It means active dedication to fulfilling the mandate before you.

- Once you know your area of coverage or term of assignment. Stay within and not outside. Faithfulness requires you to retain the place of your assignment to which God has called you.

- There must be a display of a sense of responsibility.

The watchman's mission statement in the book of Isaiah 62:6-7 requires a commitment by the commissioned. It is definitely not a one-off thing nor is it a casual one, it is obviously a laborious one, no wonder Apostle Paul describes it as a travailing act. (Galatians 4:19)

As a watchman, it would be essential to be faithful in whatever you have been given to do regardless of the size of an assignment. David, our case study, was faithful in little things when nobody was looking, even though he was not paid attention to, left alone to tend the sheep at the backside of the desert. (1 Samuel 16:11) He was consistently loyal to what he was asked to do and meanwhile the God that sees brought him from the obscurity to the limelight.

There is always a goal to be accomplished, and it requires dedication on the watchman, most times there would be nobody monitoring you.

If faithfulness is defined as consistently loyal, then to who are you expected to be loyal?

- God

- Local assembly

- The authority over you. (1 Samuel 14:1-14; 21:6-10; 26:6-16; 2 Samuel 15:21; 17-15-162 Samuel 23:16)

- Team. The ability to be loyal to your other

teammates is very important. Unity is very important with the things of God. (Psalm 133, 2 Samuel 11:6-12)

A worthy example is Epaphras, Paul testified of his commitment and faithfulness.

"You so learned it from Epaphras, our beloved fellow servant. He is a faithful minister of Christ in our stead and as our representative and yours." Colosians 1:7)

"Epaphras, who is one of yourselves, a servant of Christ Jesus, sends you greetings. [He is always striving for you earnestly in his prayers, [pleading] that you may [as persons as persons of ripe character and clear conviction] stand firm and mature [in spiritual growth], convinced and fully assured in everything willed by God." (Colossians 4:12)

- Your service must be dispensed faithfully and wholeheartedly in fear of God rather than fear of man (2 Chronicles 19:9)

- If you are convinced that you have been called into this ministry, please prove it by your faithfulness. (1 Peter 4:10)

There is a reward for faithfulness, and these rewards are:

- You will be guarded. (1 Samuel 2:9)

- You will be richly blessed. (Proverbs 28:10)

- Faithfulness provokes divine enlargement and unsolicited promotion. (1 Samuel 16:12-13; Luke 16:10:12; Luke 19:17)

- You will have blessings in due season. (Luke 12:42)

- It avails much, ushering the glory and the grace of God. (James 5:16b)

- Makes you outstanding. (Proverbs 22:29)

DILIGENCE:

"He who waits on God never waits too long." - Chuck Wagner

SCRIPTURE

"Praying always with all prayer and supplication in the Spirit, being watchful to this end with all perseverance and supplication for all the saints." (Ephesians 6:18)

Perseverance and diligence must be decisive. It involves a relentless effort to the best of your ability in getting the desired result. As a watchman, you will be receiving instruction as the plan and purpose of God about the object of watching. You must pray until something happens, or you are relieved from such burdens as God wills.

As a WATCHMAN, it is expected of you to be occupied with your assignment. (Luke 19:13) To achieve the goal of delivering God's glory, it will require laboring fervently in the place of prayer that is Paul said, "My little children, for whom I labor in birth again until Christ is formed in you." (Galatians 4:19) it was also mentioned of Epaphras, he labored fervently for others in prayers, that they may stand perfect and complete in all the will of God. (Colossians 4:12)

- You are expected to be diligent to make your call and election sure. (2 Peter 1:10)

- In this assignment, there is no stopping, no retreat. Having put your hands on the plow, you are not expected to look back. (Luke 9:62) Many people are still trapped in the dungeon of the dark kingdom who need to be evacuated. (Colossians 1:13) A watchman must pay due diligence attention not to quit when there is still a need to take action. You must never give up until there is a change or till you are relieved of the burden or assignment. (2 Corinthians 12:8-9)

- Watching under Isaiah 62:6-7 requires some length of time, which may make it discouraging to watchmen who may want to call it quit. But we must learn to commit to the task before us. (Luke 9:62) Removal of strongholds may require time.

- The King's business requires urgency. The assignment of the watchman requires that of persistent hard work. That requires diligence to meet an expected goal. Timing and effort are required. The goal is when the predetermined results are gotten.

- Perseverance is required for effectiveness in prayer. Jesus as our role model did not give up watching even when the disciples gave up. We were told, "He prayed [all the] more earnestly and intently." (Luke 22:44)

- Perseverance must be intentional and purposeful because there is a goal to be met, you cannot afford to give up. From Jesus' account, in the garden of Gethsemane, we can see a demonstration of rugged determination.

- Persistence cannot be separated from a successful work of praying. Christ taught us in Luke 18:1-8 about importunity in prayer. In that proverb, certain things bearing on persistence were noted such as urgency, intensity, force, repetition. An excellent watchman should not be a quitter, but one who must be able to ASK, until the desired result is obtained. A classic example is Elijah, who after receiving the word of God tarried in the place of prayer while everybody else feasted, to bring the word to pass. (1 Kings 18:1,41-45)

- To exhibit diligence in our praying, there must be an earnest, deep concern for the subject matter. It also requires steady and continuous effort. "Be unceasing in prayer [praying perseveringly. (Luke 18:1-8)

- "Without persistence, prayers may go unanswered.

Importunity is made up of the ability to hold on, to continue, to wait with unrelaxed and unrelaxable grasp, restless desire, and restful patience."

- Perseverance will call for sacrifice by the watchman. Time and efforts. Which means something must be forsaken.

- When matters are not pressed through it results to failure in prayer. Abraham's failure. (Genesis 18: 16-33)

- Moses denied himself food and fasted forty days and forty nights for Israel. Daniel waited for twenty one days in prayer and fasting to receive information for the deliverance of Israel from Babylon. (Daniel 10)

- Watching requires diligence, it involves earnest prayer. Definitely the prayer that brings out sweat like blood was no kind of a slothful man's prayer. Moreover when it always has to be done.(Luke 22:44)

INTEGRITY

"Integrity is not a conditional word. It doesn't blow in the wind or change with the weather. It is your inner image of yourself, and if you look in there and see a man who won't cheat, then you know he never will."
- John D. MacDonald

SCRIPTURE

"The integrity of the upright guides them, but the unfaithful are destroyed by their duplicity." Proverbs 11:3

Integrity means:

- God can depend on you not to violate the terms of your office as a WATCHMAN

- The people can depend on you not to abuse the privilege of your office.

- The team can depend on you not to break rank and or be an Achan. (1 Chronicle 12: 32-24; Joshua 7)

- Be responsible for the task assigned to you, that you would do it to the best of your God-given ability. Be able to carry the command to the letter, not half do the job. Tasks must always be finished. Until Goliath's head was cut off, David did not stop. Learn from the Rechabites who followed through on the instructions they got from their fathers 'The commands of Jonadab son of Recab to his sons have been carried out to the letter. (Jeremiah 35: 6- 19)

- You must be able to be trusted to keep confidential information. Confidentiality is an ethical principle associated with several professions (e.g., medicine, law, religion, professional psychology, and journalism)

- This information is secret, private, classified,

restricted, known only to you or a few individuals by the privilege of your office which you are not expected to reveal to anyone except otherwise instructed by God. Some people wanted to associate with me, not so much because they liked me but just to get information from me about people that they could not. Whatever information you have is just revealed to you to perform your duty. Before God does anything on earth, He does not hide from His prophets, before the destruction of Sodom and Gomorrah. God asked, *"Shall I hide from Abraham what I am about to do?"* When you have this kind of information, ask Him what you are to do with it. If it is a warning, you are to deliver to whoever, the instruction from God with wisdom, not going to town with it.

- Information should be kept until the manifestation; like when Anna and Simeon knew about the birth of Christ. They prayed without telling others about what God revealed to them.

- There is also information done or communicated to us secretly by others, it may be personal or institutional. You are not expected to share with anyone that does not have a part in it. In a normal situation, the people in the prayer ministry should be the first set of people to know about any change or any new implementation in a church setting before others to enable them to pray it through with the leadership. It will be an abuse of office to discuss with anyone who does not have business to do it regardless of their association with you.

- It will be a betrayal of trust if you pray with others in a matter concerning others and you do a personal follow up with the party involved behind the others. Don't do after prayer points with other people. For instance, prayer is raised in your team, you need not make it a prayer point with another friend anywhere else in the world. I always tell my people, "what happens in Vegas stays in Vegas. When entrusted with the confidence of another do not betray it."

- Revelations about others revealed to you should be kept confidential, even away from the party, except at God's direction should you tell. It is revealed to you that you may pray and not to boost your ego. When you have insight into a situation unknown to others, don't spread it. (Proverbs 11:13) As a WATCHMAN, you must be able to keep private and secret information, you must be able to be entrusted with private matters for individual or corporate, you must be able to keep secret matters for select groups known by your position.

- You are expected to keep privileged information from others who are not to be part of it no matter your relationship with them. When it is not public, it is not public. (Proverbs 25:9; Micah 7:5b)

- Sources of such information could be directly from God, from the leadership of your local church, your prayer team and the people over who you watch over.

- Your motives must be clear. (Proverbs 16:2) Always ensure that your motives align with the will of God. Not self –seeking or self –service.

- As a WATCHMAN, there should be no evidence of negligence or misconduct. You must be exemplary and trustworthy. (Daniel 6:4)

- Integrity is standing on your watch with or without supervision when you promise to do so. Esther did not just say, *"If I perish, I perish."* She and her maids engaged in prayer and fasting like the rest of the Jews. (Esther 4:15-16) That was a demonstration of undivided loyalty, uncompromising in belief like Paul. (Acts 21:11-14) Integrity is standing by your commitment even in the face of personal adversity and inconvenience. It is meaning what you say and not doing otherwise.

- Integrity is doing the right thing, even when nobody's watching. It is about deciding what the right thing to do is; the right choice to make and then handling that decision fairly for all concerned. Integrity is a concept of consistency of actions, values, methods, measures, principles, expectations, and outcomes. In ethics, integrity is regarded as the honesty and truthfulness of one's actions.

- Integrity can be the opposite of hypocrisy because it regards internal consistency as a virtue and suggests that parties holding apparently conflicting values should account for the discrepancy or alter their beliefs.

- The word "integrity" is derived from the Latin adjective *integer* (whole, complete). In this context, integrity is the inner sense of "wholeness" deriving from qualities such as honesty and consistency of character. One may judge that others "have integrity" if they act according to the values, beliefs, and principles they claim to hold.

HONESTY

- Honesty is telling the truth.

- Honesty is straightforward conduct.

- Honesty is being sincere, truthful, trustworthy, honorable, fair, genuine, and loyal with integrity.

According to Proverbs 12:22 "the Lord detests lying lips, but he delights in men who are truthful." An honest watchman must be able, to tell the truth, sometimes hard truth, with love and kindness.

HUMILITY

"Humility is the foundation of all the other virtues hence, in the soul in which this virtue does not exist there cannot be any other virtue except in mere appearance." - Saint Augustine

SCRIPTURE

"But he gives us more grace. That is why Scripture says: "God opposes the proud but shows favor to the humble." (James 4:6)

Humility is the quality or state of being humble. Meekness is having power but putting it under control. None can be an effective watchman in the power of the spirit without humility. God needs your partnership, but he cannot use the proud.

Humility made David run errands despite his ordination as a king. (1 Samuel 16:3, 13; 17: 17-18)

- Humility is lowering or abasing yourself in such a manner as to attain a place of lowliness. It is seeing you through God's eyes rather than our own.

- Humility is not a denial of the gift or calling of God, but the acknowledgment that the source is God's and that you are just an instrument.

- Humility helps submission to authority; possessing a servant's heart. (1 Peter 2:18)

- Humility helps to accommodate criticism. (I Peter 3:8-17)

- Humility helps one to take correction with correct perspective. (Proverb 10:17; 12:1)

- Helps in the acceptance of a lowly place. (Proverb 25:6-7)

- Helps to facilitate working with others, regardless of their status and estate.

- Help us to be good stewards.

- Quickens forgiveness and bitterness. (Matthew 18:21-35; Ephesians 4:31-32)

- Needful in serving God and more so, as a WATCHMAN. It makes teamwork easier because there is a willingness to associate with others. (Micah 6:) It does not make you ignorant or ignore your gift (Ephesians 3:8)

- Doesn't stop you from taking necessary actions. (Matthew 21:12; Mark 11:15-16)

- Humility is an essential virtue required in the life and ministry of a watchman for him to succeed in his assignment since the watchman cannot work independently of God. (Psalm127:1 -2) God cannot accommodate the proud. Grace is a must, to do the work of the watchman.(Zechariah 12:10) And grace is from God. Humility draws grace for the recipient. (James 4:6)

- To be an effective Watchman, one must be humble and not domineering.

- Prayer time is never a time to create an impression or show off. So, don't be domineering. I have heard people coming to lead prayers, and people hail them to show them; hailing deliberately demanded by the one to lead.

- Don't seek for promotion or recognition. The physical promotion will not do you any good in this work. It is not about your title, it is about the anointing and the power that God bestows on you as you work with him in the closet.

• Humility is essential to work harmoniously among a team of watchmen. (Philippians 2:3-7)

For Further study: Luke 18:9-14; Romans 12:16; Ephesians 4:2; James s 4:6; 1 Chronicles 7:14; Philippians 2:5-8; 1 Peter 5:5; Proverbs 16:18-19; Psalm: 119:21; 147:6; Proverbs 18:12

PURITY

"The way to preserve the peace of the Church is to preserve its purity. " - Matthew Henry

SCRIPTURE

"Those who cleanse themselves from the latter will be instruments for special purposes, made holy, useful to the Master and prepared to do any good work." (2 Timothy 2:21)

As a Watchman, watching over others and in deep hunger and thirst of excellence in ministry, one of the cardinal things you will need to imbibe is Purity. Purity will need to come before power. Naomi advised Ruth to *"Wash and anoint herself."* (Ruth 3: 3). Why is this necessary? The Watchman goes before God on behalf of others, and nobody goes before Him in iniquity. Purity is freedom from anything that corrupts, contaminates or pollutes the body, the soul or the spirit. (Zechariah 3:1-7; 2 Corinthians 7:1; 1

Thessalonians 5:23)

We, therefore, must endeavor to keep ourselves clean and set ourselves apart in holiness.

David asked:

"Who shall go up into the mountain of the Lord? Or who shall stand in His Holy Place? He who has clean hands and a pure heart, who has not lifted himself up to falsehood or to what is false, nor sworn deceitfully. He shall receive blessing from the Lord and righteousness from the God of his salvation." (Psalm 24:3-5)

"No one can become a high priest simply because he wants such an honor. He must be called by God for his work, just as Aaron was. That is why Christ did not honor himself by assuming he could become high priest. No, he was chosen by God, who said to him, "You are my son. Today I have become your father." (Hebrews 5:4-5)

- As a priest in the model of the High Priest, Jesus, one must be pure, holy, blameless, unstained, by sin, separated from sinners. (Hebrews 7:26)

- You must flee from touching things that defile such as the gold, the glory, and the girls. You must abstain from foolishness, flattery. Learn to apply wisdom in all circumstances. (Revelation 14:4 Judges 16; James 3:17;1 John 2:16)

- You must maintain a pure heart for God loves

those who are pure in heart and will only partner with such. (Jeremiah 17:9-10; [Proverbs 22:11; 4:23-27; Matthew 5:8)

- You must maintain purity in your body, it houses the spirit of God, and that is on whom you rely on doing your assignment. (1 Corinthians 6:16-20; John 14; 16; 26; Roman 8:26; Judges 16) Defiling the body is an invitation to the departure of the Holy Spirit from your life, you don't want to be like Samson. Flee from flirting. (Judges 16:20-21)

- You must maintain purity in speech. (Psalms 12:2; Proverbs 10:19)

- You are expected to be pure in conduct and in a relationship with others. (2 Timothy 2:22)

- You are expected to be pure in the spirit. (2 Corinthians 7:1)

- You are expected to be pure in your thoughts and conscience. (Philippians 4:8; Titus 1:15)

How can you maintain purity?

- By taking heed and keeping watch on yourself according to the word of God. You cannot afford to be careless. Carelessness will only lead to destruction just like it happened to Samson. (Psalm 119:9;2 Samuel 22:27)

- You must give no room for iniquity, defending or

rationalizing it. (Psalm 66:18; 1 Peter 1:16)

- Learn to flee from any appearances of evil. (Genesis 39:6-12;1 Thessalonians 5:22-23)

- You must be determined to maintain your purity. (Daniel 1:8 Hebrews 12:14)

Purity

- Grants you the privilege of partnering with God to accomplish His purpose on earth. (Matthew 5:8)

- Boldness to approach God. (1 John 3:21-22)

- It creates ways to escape from much temptation. (1 Corinthians 10:13)

- Purity makes prayer powerful and impactful. (James 5:16)

- Purity is a confidence booster. (Psalm 66:18-22)

- There is the elimination of biases or prejudice.

- It enables divine protection. (2 Kings 6:14-16)

Impurity is a:

- Stopper. (Zechariah 3:1-7)

- Blocker. (Isaiah 58; Proverbs 15:8, 29)

For further study: Ephesians 5:1-3; Hebrew 10:22-24; Galatians 5:19-21;1 John 3:3

OBEDIENCE

"Just as a servant knows that he must first obey his master in all things, so the surrender to an implicit and unquestionable obedience must become the essential characteristics of our lives." - Andrew Murray

SCRIPTURE

"We demolish arguments and every pretension that sets itself up against the knowledge of God, and we take captive every thought to make it obedient to Christ. And being ready to punish all disobedience when your obedience is fulfilled." (2 Corinthians 10:5-6)

A watchman must learn how to practice obedience. Knowing you did not call yourself as such you have to obey the master

"I have posted watchmen on your walls, O Jerusalem: they will never be silent day or night. You, who call on the lord, give yourselves no rest. And give him no rest till establishes Jerusalem and makes her the praise of the earth." (Isaiah 62:6-7)

What is obedience? It is doing God's will.

Obedience should be a hallmark of a watchman.

Obedience is compliance, agreement, submission, respect, conformity to a known will a superior being. (1 Samuel 15:22; John 14:21; John 15:10)

Do you not know that if you continually surrender

yourselves to anyone to do his will, you are the slaves of him whom you obey, whether that be to sin, which leads to death, or to obedience which leads to righteousness (right doing and right standing with God)? (Romans 6:16; Romans 7:6; 2 Corinthians 10:6) A watchman must learn how to practice obedience. Knowing you did not call yourself as such you have to obey the master.

What is obedience? It is doing God's will.

Why do we need to obey?

- It is a demonstration of faith.

- It is a demonstration of love.

Benefit:

- Allows the full operation of the Holy Spirit. (John 14:15-16)

- Access to the things of the spirit.

- Guarantee response to our prayer. (1 John 3:22)

- Facilitate speedy answers to prayers.

- Learning obedience must come before learning to pray. To obey is better than sacrifice. (1 Samuel 15:22)

- Compliance with the word and instruction of God. (John 14:23 24; John 15: 10)

- Acting on His express instructions. (Jeremiah

7:23)

- Walking in the law of God. (Deuteronomy 11: 27; Isaiah 42:24)

- It is a demonstration of love.

- It is a demonstration of faith.

- It is action based on trust. (Hebrews 11:6)

- Willingness to submit.

- The act of pleasing God. ([1 John 3:21-24)

- Compliance with laid down rules.

Who are you expected to obey?

- God, the Father, the Son, and the Holy Spirit. (1 John 2: 3-6; Romans 6:16; Romans 7:6 Acts 5:32 Roman 8:14; Joshua 1:8;1 Corinthians 2:9-10)

- Spiritual leaders. (Ephesians 6:1; Hebrews 13:17)

- Government (Romans 13:1-3; Titus 3:1)

When there is a conflict with the commandment of God and the instruction from the sphere and cadre of leadership; you have to follow God's.(Acts 5:29) Failure to do so may cause fatal disaster. (1 king 13:1-28) The key to success is the ability to hear and listen to God convincingly.

You must also learn how to wait on the Lord without rushing into anything and to know how to take things back to Him for clarity and clearance.

For instance, as a watchman over a local assembly, if you receive an express instruction from God concerning a matter, don't rush to inform your leader. Inquire again and again, and if there is an objection wait and pray again that your leader will see what you see or hear what you hear. For me, I had learned not to rush to my Pastor whenever I receive such instructions. I make sure I pray over it and convinced that it is from God. Most of the time, by the time I get to him; there is an agreement, because he must have perceived the same revelation at that point. If it is God, all things will always work together in His own time.

- True obedience does not delay, it goes straight into action.

- Delayed obedience is disobedience.

- Doing the small things and the big ones.

- Asking questions when you are not sure of the instructions.

- Obedience does not require full understanding. You are not always going to receive beyond what you are commanded to do. (Genesis 12:4)

- Going all the way. Unreserved. (Joshua 11:15; 22:2-3)

- Better than sacrifice. (1 Samuel 15:13-24)

- Should be from the heart. (Deuteronomy 11:13; Romans 6:17)

- It is marked by cheerful service and willingness. (Isaiah 1:19)

- It means not deviating from the words of the command of God. (Deuteronomy 28:14; Luke 2:39; Numb e r s 2 0 : 12)

- Obedience must be instant and constant. (Philippians 2:12)

- Partial obedience is disobedience. (Jonah 1)

- Disobedience results in an effort in futility. (Luke 6:46-49)

- Disobedience will reject service and person of the watchman by God. (1 Samuel 15:28-29)

- Disobedience will cause destruction. (Deuteronomy 30:17-18; 1 king 13; Joshua 7)

- Disobedience will cause a curse (Deuteronomy 11:28; Ephesians 5:6)

- Disobedience can terminate appointment (1 Samuel 13:13-14)

BENEFITS OF OBEDIENCE

It is good :

- For protection. (Proverbs 19:16)

- For preservation. (Deuteronomy 7:12)

- For perpetuity. (Deuteronomy 5:29;1 king 3:14)

- For direction. (Roman 8:14)

- For possession. (Exodus 19:5)

- For promotion. (Deuteronomy 28:1)

- For prosperity. (Job 36:11)

- For development. ([John 7:17)

- For divine presence. (Zechariah 3:7)

- For victory. (2 Corinthians 10:6)

- For fullness of operating in the Holy Spirit.

- To access the things of the spirit. (1 John 3:22)

- To guarantee response to our prayer.

- To facilitate speedy answers to prayers.

Learning obedience must come before learning to pray. To obey is better than sacrifice. (1 Samuel 15:22)

When you have to work as a team in a local setting or as occasion demands, you have to work under authority and be accountable. You must be a tithe payer. You must be subject to your church /team leadership.

BOLDNESS

"Boldness comes in the face of threat, "Courage faces fear and thereby masters it, Cowardice represses fear and is thereby mastered by it." - Martin Luther King, Jr.

SCRIPTURE

"And when they had prayed, the place where they had gathered together was shaken, and they were all filled with the Holy Spirit and began to speak the Word of God with boldness." (Acts 4:31)

Without opposition or threats you will probably not need boldness and courage, but in this work, you will encounter ferocious beings. (Ephesians 6:12; Luke 10:19) You will meet the Pharaohs, and the Herods of this world would want to resist the work. Jesus has promised He would build His church and the gates of Hades shall not prevail against it. (Matthew 16:18) In doing this, He needs human partners. If there were no opposition, there would be no need for God's charge to Joshua, to be courageous. (Joshua 1:6-7,9)

- You must be audacious and brave to face opposition and drive out illegal occupants. (1 Corinthians 16:9; Numbers 33:52,55)

- There would always be giants along this part, but giants falls. (1 Chronicles 20:6-7; Romans 8:33-39)

- It is fearless in the face of danger. You must be

bold to fight against evil intimidation. Spiritual warfare has nothing to do with age or gender. David was as bold as a lion and did not allow the enemy's threat to destroy his confidence. (1 Samuel 17:8-10, 23-25, 32-51; Jeremiah 1:7-8)

- As a WATCHMAN, often, you will be used of God to relay messages, "Thus says the Lord." To others, who may be older or senior in rank to you, so boldness is needful. (1 Samuel 3:10:18;2 Samuel 12:1-15; Ezekiel 3; 33:3,7)

- It requires boldness to fight against opposition; people who can easily be intimidated are not fit to be Watchmen. (Judges 7:1-9) It required boldness for Elijah to face the prophets of Baal at a ratio of 1:450

- It requires boldness to evacuate illegal occupants, that was why Joshua was encouraged to be strong, and of good courage, it would not be a bread and butter thing to resist the gates of Hades. (Ephesians 6:11-12;2 Corinthians 10:3-4; Joshua 1:6,7,9)

- A watchman is a warrior! And a warrior must be bold and not timid. (2 Timothy 1:7)

- Boldness will require taking a risk when it doesn't make sense. But before you take any audacious risk, ask yourself, "on whose order?

How to acquire boldness

- Through the word. (Joshua 1:8)

- Prayer. (Acts 4:29,31)

- Trust in God. (1 Samuel 17:37; Daniel 3:16-18)

- It is rooted and grounded in faith, in God, and empowered by the Holy Spirit. (Acts 2:4,39;4:8)

- Experience. (1 Samuel 17:32-36)

- Praise.

Benefits of Boldness

- It makes you stay on your course and not retreat.

- It strengthens you for the battles before you that you might finish your course.

PATIENCE

"Patience is not about waiting, but the ability to keep a good attitude while waiting." - Anonymous

SCRIPTURE

"For the vision is yet for an appointed time and it hastens to the end [fulfilment]; it will not deceive or disappoint. Though it tarry, wait [earnestly] for it, because it will surely come; it will not be behindhand on its appointed day." (Habakkuk 2:3)

Patience is a needed attribute that WATCHMAN who desires to leave behind an indelible mark, you cannot afford to do without. Patience is needful because you will be dealing with different people and issues, and time is involved. The length which you cannot determine except God.

Patience is a state of endurance under difficult circumstances which can persevere in the face of delay or provocation without acting on annoyance or anger in a negative or exhibiting forbearance when under strain. Especially when faced with longer-term difficulties.

Patience is the level of endurance one's character can take before negativity. It is also used to refer to the character trait of being steadfast, or which you can wait for things.

Patience is required because the assignment is not tangible, and the result may not be visible as quickly as human wants. It can attract criticism and causes frustration, the attribute patience will help guard against that. One of the earliest warnings that God gave me when I took over my assignment in May 2005 was "Let neither accolade nor criticism distracts you from which I have called you to do." My watchword has been to ignore either and also to develop patience with myself and others. Is it easy? No, for criticism came from every quarter and opposition rising within and without, but one that kept me going and that would keep you going is "Looking away from [from all that will distract to Jesus, who is the Leader and the Source of our faith giving the first incentive for our belief and is also its Finisher bringing it to maturity and perfection. He for the joy of obtaining the prize] that was set before Him, endured the cross, despising and ignoring the shame, and is now seated at the right hand of the throne of God." (Hebrews 12:2)

"For God is not unrighteous to forget or overlook your labor and the love which you have shown for His name's sake in ministering to the needs of the saints (His own consecrated people), as you still do. But we do [strongly and earnestly] desire for each of you to show the same diligence and sincerity [all the way through] in realizing and enjoying the full assurance and development of [your] hope until the end, In order that you may not grow disinterested and become [spiritual] sluggards, but imitators, behaving as do those who through faith (by their leaning of the entire personality on God in Christ in absolute trust and confidence in His power, wisdom, and goodness And by practice of patient endurance and waiting are now inheriting the promises." (Hebrews 6:10-12)

What could be the factor that made David wait that long after his ordination to assume the kingship office? It must have been a virtue called PATIENCE. Patience is endurance, staying power, tolerance, fortitude, and serenity. It took twenty years for the coronation to be implemented; so, in praying and interceding over a matter as a watchman it may be quick as we may want, there would be obvious opposition like Goliath that could be gotten rid of easily and there would also be the oblivious oppositions like Saul that you have to tackle for longer periods. For the institution to be established a praise, there would be attack even from your team, so get ready.(1 Samuel 30: 6)

You must be able to endure provocation, annoyance, misfortune, or pain with calm and strength.

As a WATCHMAN, you must tolerate delay; responses from God may take some time to come, but you just have to learn to wait and not go ahead of God. Will you run ahead of God even after you have asked like David asked; "Shall I pursue" and you are yet to receive an answer, what will you do? Take matters into your own hands like Saul or wait still? (1 Samuel 15)

You first must have patience with yourself, things may not evolve as you desire, and you may not be where you think you should be, even in your assignment, the secret to success is leaning on God and doing one thing at a time. Don't bite more than you can chew. (Psalm 40:1; Proverbs 3:5-6)

It is the plan of God and not your plan; it's the Lord's purpose and not yours, so you need not fret over it. Don't be under any pressure or anxiety, He knows how and when to bring His purpose to pass. (Isaiah 46:10-11)

Patience is a demonstration of our faith in God's timing and power, and it is also needful because offenses are inevitable. Unfair treatment will abound. Elijah is an example of a watchman that by patience did not give up despite delay to his request (James 5:17-18; 1 king 17:1; 1 king 18:42-45)

Sources of Patience

- Through faith.(Romans 5:1)

- It is the fruit of the spirit.(Galatians 5:22-23)

- It is developed through hardship.(Romans 5:3; James 1:3-4)

- It comes through our relationship with God. (Revelations 14:12)

- Through God's power and goodness. (Colossians 1:11)

Benefits of Patience

- Patience creates confidence

- Patience encourages decisions that results in success.

- It helps you to overlook fault in others and therefore enable you to pray for others without considering their fault, and it also helps you to work with others successfully. (Colossians 3:12-13;1 Thessalonians 5:14; Ephesians 4:2)

- It produces endurance in the face of trials and persecution. (Revelation 14:12)

- Patience releases the staying power in the place of prayer while waiting for the manifestation of promise. (Romans 8:25)

- Patience guarantees the security of the inheritance. (Hebrews 6:12; 10:36; James 5:7; Psalm 37:34)

- Patience will get you to the finish line, not only in your assignment but also in your Christian race. (Hebrew 12:1;2 Timothy 4:7)

- Patience exposes deception.

- Patience is a catalyst for strength. (Psalm 27;14)

- It produces a response to prayers. (Psalm 40:1)

- Patience eliminates weariness associated with working around unappreciative people. (Galatians 6:9)

- Patience is a Hope booster.

- Impatience only breeds anxiety, fears, discouragement, and ultimately failure.

TEACHABLE

"To be conscious that you are ignorant of the fact is a great step to knowledge." - Benjamin Disraeli

SCRIPTURE

"Let the wise hear and increase in learning, and the one who understands obtains guidance." (Proverbs 1:5)

A WATCHMAN that desires to pursue a successful path in their assignment must ordinarily be teachable, apt, and willing to learn, open to teachings. And eager to learn.

Nobody knows it all, that is why it is essential to apply your mind to instructions and corrections and your eras to the word of knowledge. (Proverbs 23:12, 23)

You must be a person that will be submissive to instructions and discipline. You must love instruction and discipline. Obey the instruction of your teachers and be submissive to instructors.

Why is learning necessary

- Lack of instruction brings death.

- A teachable heart is needful for a successful performance

- Increase in skill and soundness in the discharge of duty. It produces mastery and maturity. (Proverbs 1:5)

- Learning is a process. You can never stop learning, for there is always more to learn. You must never get to a point where you get satisfied with your achievement. (Philippians 3:12-14; Proverbs 19:27)

- Learning helps growth. when growth stops, decay begins.

- You must aspire to learn some new things about your assignment, especially something you ought to know but do not know. It gives you a different perspective and especially the right one that enhances the effectiveness and efficiency of your assignment.

- Learning is not restricted to one source, you can learn from your experience; both the good and the bad.

- Be open to reading from others through their books.

- Be open to suggestions and corrections, especially constructive criticisms.

- Being teachable will open you up for wisdom beyond you. (Proverbs 12:1)

- Lack of a teachable spirit can cause redundancy and inefficiency in the discharge of duty and repetitive mistakes.

- Struggling without understanding. (Acts 8:31)

We can be teachable through the following:

- The Holy Spirit. The Holy Spirit teaches us reveals things to us we do not know about. The Holy Spirit is the best teacher.

- The experienced leaders.

- Through personal past mistakes and mistakes of others regardless of their position as superior or subordinate or even from outside of your team like Jethro to Moses. (Exodus 18:14-27) be open-minded to learn from others regardless of their status compared to yours

- The word of God. (2 Timothy 3:16)

- The written books by others

- Deliberate mentorship.

HOW TO BE TEACHABLE

- There must be a desire and willingness

- There must be a submission

- There must be an acknowledgment of weakness. (Acts 8:30-31)

- Ask, listen, and act to instructions.

- Careful observation. (Luke 11:1)

"A scoffer seeks Wisdom in vain [for his very attitude blinds and deafens him to it], but knowledge is easy to him who [being teachable] understands." (Proverbs 14:6)

Example: David asks God to show him the way (Psalm 25:4-5; 27:11; 86:11; 143:10] The disciples were not ashamed to ask Jesus to teach them to pray. [Luke

11:1)

Identifying un-teachable spirit

- Resistance to change even when it is beneficial to the well-being of the recipient.

- It is usually a byproduct of pride.

- It may be an indication of ignorance.

- Cover up for foolishness.

- Fear of the unknown.

- I know it all attitude.

- Holy Spirit will teach me. (1 Timothy 4:11-16;2 Timothy 2:2)

- It is cancerous. (Matthew 16:6-11)

SELF CONTROL

"I am, indeed, a king, because I know how to rule myself." - Pietro Aretino

SCRIPTURE

"But I discipline my body and keep it under control, lest after preaching to others I myself should be disqualified." (1 Corinthians 9:27)

As WATCHMAN one of your roles would be that of a warrior. Warriors fight in battles, without battles there would be no warfare, and that means you are a soldier in the Lord's army and such it would be expected of you to subject yourself to certain control as not to inhibit your duty. Apostles Paul, for instance, admonishes Timothy the mentee that, "No soldier when in service gets entangled in the enterprises of civilian life; his aim is to satisfy and please the one who enlisted him."

Self –control is the ability to control your habit and lifestyle. It is the ability to control your emotions, behavior, and desires, especially towards the desired goal. It is the ability to control your own behavior, especially in terms of reactions and responses to people and issues. It is the ability to rule your personal life, so it is not driven by the desires of the flesh, the desires of the eyes or the pride of life. (1 John 2:16) It is the ability to control passion, pleasure, and pride in driving your activities.

"For the flesh lusteth against the spirit, and the spirit against the flesh: and these are contrary the one to the other: so that ye cannot do the things that ye would." (Galatians 5:17)

- Manner of speech. You must watch over your speech, too many of words will make you divulge privileged and confidential information. You must be a person of few words. (1 Timothy 4:12; Matthew 12 :34, 36-37; James 1:19-20)

- Time management. You must control your time,

prioritizing tasks according to purpose. (Ephesians 5:15-16; John 9: 4 Hebrews 12:1; 1 Peter 2:11; Galatians 5:24; 17, James 3:1-13)

- Appetite control. (Proverbs 23:1-3;1 king 18:42)

- Desires and pleasures. (Judges 16; Colossians 3:5)

BENEFITS OF SELF CONTROL

- It helps in personal sacrifice to achieve a godly purpose. Esther sacrificed the pleasure and comfort of the palace for the deliverance of her people. (Esther 4) There it may not be comfortable or convenient to do certain things in your watching, but you have to do it anywhere.

- Secured victory

How to achieve self-control

- Deliberate and determined. (Daniel 1:8 -10)

- Faith in Christ. (1 Thessalonians 4:1-12)

- Scriptural instruction. (Ephesians 4:22-24)

- Engaging weapons of warfare. (2 Corinthians 10:3-5; Ephesians 6:10-18; Colossians 2:20-23)

- Godly discipline. (Genesis 39:7-9; Galatians 5:17)

- By the grace of God. We need the unmerited favor of God (Titus 2:11-14)

REFLECTIONS

- Can you identify any area of deficiency?

- What steps would you take to overcome that?

- Take action now.

CHAPTER 5
THE GUIDING PRINCIPLES

"He who floats with current, who does not guide himself according to higher principles, who has no ideal, no convictions- such a man is a mere article of the world's furniture -a -thing moved, instead of a living and moving being - an -echo, not a voice." - Henri Frederic Amiel

"And you will know the truth, and the truth will set you free." (John 8:32)

There are things you cannot afford to do away with or not have because of their vitality to the success of your assignment. To have a victorious, fruitful, and prosperous ministry, you just have to engage in these practices.

Intimacy with God

- Your appointment and assignments are not initiated by you, so to progress in this call you have to depend totally on God. If Jesus was close to the Father, you also have to be close to Him. For all the prophets of old, they did nothing without direction. To know his plans, therefore you have to be in constant fellowship with Him. David was in constant fellowship with God.

"Deep calls unto deep at the noise of your waterfalls; All Your waves and billows have gone over me." (Psalm 42:7)

- As a Watchman, you have to be a mountaintop, tent, and altar person. Let us consider examples in the scripture; Moses (Exodus 17:15; 33:7-11) Joshua (Exodus 33:11) Elijah (1 king 18:32) and ultimately Jesus (Luke 6:12; Luke 9:28) not surprisingly, Joshua succeeded Moses, he was a young man that always tarries back in the tent with Moses (Exodus 33:11)

- You must not be afraid to be alone. Jesus always withdrew himself to pray alone. Just to be with the Father. (Matthew 14:23) No wonder He did exactly as the Father would have expected of Him.

"So Jesus answered them by saying, I assure you, most solemnly I tell you, the Son is able to do nothing of

Himself (of His own accord); but He is able to do only what He sees the Father doing, for whatever the Father does is what the Son does in the same way [in His turn]. The Father dearly loves the Son and discloses to (shows) Him everything that He Himself does. And He will disclose to Him (let Him see) greater things yet than these, so that you may marvel and be full of wonder and astonishment." (John 5:19-20)

As we can observe from the above passage, Jesus made us to understand that without intimacy with God the Father, there was no way He could have done that much work of healings, deliverance, and miracles as He did. Therefore, as a Christian and much more as a watchman, who stands in gap for others, one art we must learn and perfect, is the art of being alone with God.

How do we get intimate with God?

The watchman burdens originate from God; therefore, intimacy with the Father is indispensable. The question now, is how do I get intimate with God? Intimacy with God must be intentional and decisive (Psalm 27:4) and it requires time and effort (Psalm 42:1 -2; 63: 1-2) One can grow in intimacy with God, the more you draw closer to Him the more He draws closer to you (James 4:8)

We get intimate with God through these ways and more.

- **Prayer:**

Prayer is essential oil to the engine for the watchman, it's the major thing we do. God wants us to seek him with all of our hearts; He is interested in having a relationship with us. Prayer is a form of communication with God. He wants us to communicate with him always. Prayer is listening to God; Prayer is enjoying the presence of God. *"Then you will call on me and come and pray to me, and I will listen to you. You will seek me and find me when you seek me with all your heart. I will be found by you declares the Lord."* (Jeremiah 29:12-14)

It is the will of God for His Chosen. *"Rejoice always, pray continually, give thanks in all circumstances: for this is God's will for you in Christ Jesus."* (1 Thessalonians 5: 16 -17)

The place of prayer is the place of finding help for our assignment, apart from praying for others. *"Let us approach God throne of grace with confidence, so that we may receive mercy and find grace to help us in our time of need."* (Hebrews 4:16)

- **Worship:**

How can worship enhance the art of intimacy with God? To worship is to adore, revere, exalt, honor, and magnify the Almighty God. Worship is to honor God with extravagant love and extreme submission. God enjoys true worship; True worship is centered on the person of God Worship is to recognize and express the worthiness of God and to respond to that worthiness.

(Isaiah 29:13; Matthew 15:8-9; Revelations 4:11; 5:12)

Worship can also be described as an attitude of gratitude, starting with a heart full of gratitude, springing from the depths of meditation of God's greatness and worthiness.

Worship is not just in songs but also an attitude (Deuteronomy 6:5) and the totality of your relationship with God, *"All has been heard; the end of the matter is: Fear God [revere and worship Him, knowing that He is] and keep His commandments, for this is the whole of man [the full, original purpose of his creation, the object of God's providence, the root of character, the foundation of all happiness, the adjustment to all inharmonious circumstances and conditions under the sun] and the whole [duty] for every man."* (Ecclesiastes 12:13)

Worship brings down the presence of God (Psalm 22:3; Isaiah 64: 1-3)

Worship magnifies the power of God against the presence of obstacles or anything that stands as mountains or giants before you and the people for whom you stand in gap, and therefore grants you boldness, confidence and victory like David in his confrontation with Goliath (1 Samuel 17: 36 -46) David a perfect example of a worshiper. He was a habitual worshiper. To be intimate with God is to be a true worshipper of God.

We heard him declare, "I will worship toward Your

holy temple and praise Your name for Your loving-kindness and for Your truth and faithfulness; for You have exalted above all else, your name and Your word and You have magnified Your Word above all Your name." (Psalm 138:2)

Note that God does not listen to sinners; but if anyone is God-fearing and a worshiper of Him and does His will, He listens to him. God requires true worshippers to worship the Father in spirit and in truth. (John 4:23; John 9:31)

Worship has its own benefits; some of which shall be enumerated below:

- The revelation of the will of God. "While they were worshiping the Lord and fasting, the Holy Spirit said, *"Separate now for Me Barnabas and Saul for the work to which I have called them."* (Acts 13: 2)

- Praise is a pathway to victory and guarantees the assurance of victory in battles. (Psalm 149; 2 Chronicles 20; Acts 16:25-26)

- Worship enhances our efficiency and effectiveness in the place of prayer and as intercessors. (James 5:16)

- Praise provokes God's presence. (Psalm 22:3 Isaiah 64:1-3)

- **Meditation:**

To meditate is to think deeply about what God has said to us in the scripture and applying everything that we have learned in our individual lives and to our circumstances. Meditation helps us to prepare our hearts for prayers. Meditating gives us more understanding of the Word we have learned and makes it possible for the word to dwell in our hearts. The bible talks about meditation in the bible verses below for better understanding.

"This Book of the Law shall not depart out of your mouth, but you shall meditate on it day and night that you may observe and do according to all that is written in it. For then you shall make your way prosperous, and then you shall deal wisely and have good success." (Joshua 1:8)

"But his delight and desire are in the law of the Lord, and on His law (the precepts, the instructions, the teachings of God) he habitually meditates (ponders and studies) by day and by night." (Psalm 1:2)

"Before embarking on the business of the day for instructions and directions." (Psalms 119:148)

- **Studying the Word of God**

Intimacy through the word of God is so important and essential to us as Watchmen. We can't be effective in our calling if we do not know the bible or study the bible effectively. The solution to every challenge or to any question is in the word of God. There is no prayer without the Word. Many can preach without prayer, but prayer without the Word is vain.

"For the word of God is alive and active. Sharper than any double-edged sword, it penetrates even to the dividing soul and spirit, joints and marrow; it judges the thought and the attitudes of the heart." (Hebrews 4:12)

"Your word is a lamp for my feet, a light on my path." (Psalm 119:105)

"Therefore, everyone who hears these words of mine and puts them into practice is like a wise man who built his house on the rock." (Matthew 7:24)

"In the beginning was the word and the word was with God, and the word was God." (John 1:1)

RESULT OF INTIMACY

- It is a place of receiving instruction and guidance on what to do. (Psalm 5:3; John 5:19; 8:28; 15:15; 17:7; 12:49)

"And the Lord spoke to Moses face to face, as a man speaks to his friend. Moses returned to the camp, but his minister Joshua son of Nun, a young man, did not depart from the [temporary prayer] tent." (Exodus 33:11)

No wonder Joshua became the successor to Moses. He loved staying behind in the tent.

- It is a place of opportunity to make diligent search and inquiry into what you ought to know, but you don't know or you are not sure of ([Jeremiah 33:3; Deuteronomy 13:14; 17:4) David is an example of man that inquired and repeatedly inquired from God before embarking on battles (1 Samuel 23:2,4;30:8; 2 Samuel 2:1;5:19,23) Jehoshaphat (1 Kings 22:5.) Ezra (Ezra 7:10; 24:6)

- It is a place of receiving vital and privileged information unknown to others. For vital disclosures, you must be intimate with God (Amos 3:7] Other examples are Noah (Genesis 6:13) Abraham [Genesis 18:17) Joseph [Genesis 41:30] Daniel (Daniel 2:19-23;922)

INTIMACY WITH JESUS

The position of Jesus to us is that of mediator, advocate, and intercessor just as we stand as an earthly advocate for others, so is Jesus the heavenly and eternal advocate. (Hebrews 1:3)

Our relationship with Jesus gives us the right and privilege to use His name and that name every knee standing against your operations and activities shall come down. (John 16:23-24; Philippians 2:9 -10)

We pray to God in the name of Jesus. (Ephesians 3:14-15)

We use the authority in the name of Jesus to destroy the work of the devil (Mark 16:17-18; Luke 10:19)

With that name, we lose the souls of men from the grip of the devil. (Matthew 19:19)

In the name of Jesus, poisons are neutralized from our system. (Mark 16:18)

In that name, we get the sick healed. (Mark 16:18)

Intimacy with the Holy Spirit

The Holy Spirit is our most valuable helper in the place of prayer; the Holy Spirit helps us to intercede. Jesus promised us that Helper, and He is here. He is the third person of the Trinity who helps our weaknesses and inadequacies in the place of prayer. (Roman 8:26)

"But the Comforter (Counselor, Helper, Intercessor, Advocate, Strengthener, Standby), the Holy Spirit, Whom the Father will send in My name [in My place, to represent Me and act on My behalf], He will teach you all things. And He will cause you to recall (will remind you of, bring to your remembrance) everything I have told you." (John 14:26)

- The Holy Spirit helps us to pray the right prayer according to the will of God. (James 4:1-3; Romans 8:26 -28)

The Spirit of grace for supplication is the lubricant that makes the prayer work easy, "And I will pour on the house of David and on the inhabitants of Jerusalem the Spirit of grace and supplication..." (Zechariah 12:10)

- By the Spirit of grace, Apostle Paul made a claim on the ability to do all things including prayer;

prayer is labor, and it requires grace not just to provoke but also to sustain it (1 Corinthians 15:10; Philippians 4:13; Galatians 4:19)

- Through the Holy Spirit, we learn to get through God's mind and His plans and purposes, not just for us but for places and people over whom we watch. (1 Corinthians 2:9-11) To enjoy this privilege, you have to draw closer to the Holy Spirit and be full of the Holy Spirit. An example is when the Holy Spirit Spoke about the plans of God for Paul and Barnabas in Acts 13 verses 2-3 *"While they were worshiping the Lord and fasting, the Holy Spirit said, separate now for Me Barnabas and Saul for the work to which I have called them."*

- Holy Spirit empowers us for service including the service as a WATCHMAN "But you shall receive power (ability, efficiency, and might) when the Holy Spirit has come upon you, and you shall be my witnesses in Jerusalem and all Judea and Samaria and to the ends (the very bounds) of the earth." (Acts 1:8) *"Confess to one another, therefore, your faults (your slips, your false steps, your offenses, your sins) and pray [also] for one another, that you may be healed and restored [to a spiritual tone of mind and heart]. The earnest (heartfelt, continued) prayer of a righteous man makes tremendous power available [dynamic in* its working]" (James 5:16-17)

- From the Holy Spirit Spiritual gifts comes from *"In his grace God has given us different gifts for doing certain things well. So, if God has given you the ability to prophesy, speak out with much faith has God has given you"* (Romans 12:6) *"There are different kinds of spiritual gifts, but the same spirit is the source of them all. There are different services, but we serve the same lord. God works in different ways, but it is the same God who does the work in all of us"* (1 Corinthians 12:4-6)

- Holy Spirit is the dispenser of the unction to function as a WATCHMAN. *"But you have been anointed by [you hold a sacred appointment from, you have been given an unction from] the Holy One, and you all know [the Truth], or you know all things."* (1 John 2:20)

- From the Holy Spirit, we have the anointing. *"The Spirit of the LORD is upon me, because he has anointed me to preach the gospel to the poor; he has sent me to heal the brokenhearted, to proclaim liberty to the captives and recovery of sight to the blind, to set at liberty those who are oppressed; {19} to proclaim the acceptable year of the LORD."* (Luke 4:18)

  1. The anointing is given to preach the gospel to the poor.

  2. The anointing is given to heal and restore people.

3. The anointing is given to proclaim freedom to the captives.

4. The anointing is given to open blind eyes.

5. The anointing is given to set people free.

6. The anointing flows in God's timing and proclaims God's timing.

Ways to be connected to the Holy Spirit.

- Through effective communication with the Holy Spirit.

- Being alone with God.

- Practicing His presence.

- Personal time.

- Worship

- Word

- Holiness

- Fasting and Prayer

CHAPTER 6
MANY KINDS OF PRAYERS

MANY KINDS OF PRAYERS

Jesus instructed the disciples to watch and pray; that tells immediately there can be no WATCH without praying.

"All of you must keep awake (give strict attention, be cautious and active) and watch and pray, that you may not come into temptation. The spirit indeed is willing, but the flesh is weak." (Matthew 26:41)

When God said. "I have posted watchmen, who were not to keep silent." But calling on Him, suggests prayer. In the time of Nehemiah, as they continue to watch for the enemies incursion and attack, they continued calling on God through prayer.

"But because of them we made our prayer to our God and set a watch against them day and night." (Nehemiah 4:9)

Since Prayer cannot be separated from watching let's talk about it. I will not talk about what prayers is, but all manners of prayers at your disposal and for what purpose.

Apostle Paul instructed us to pray all manner of prayers -

"Pray at all times (on every occasion, in every season) in the Spirit, with all [manner of] prayer and entreaty. To that end keep alert and watch with strong purpose and perseverance, interceding in behalf of all the saints (God's consecrated people.)" (Ephesians 6:18)

It's not just enough to know what kinds of prayer is available, but for efficacy and profiting it is necessary to know the principle that governs them. Prayer is labor in all labor, there is profit or expectation of profit. (Proverbs 14:23)

- PRAYER OF AGREEMENT:

"Again, I tell you, if two of you on earth agree (harmonize together, make a symphony together) about whatever [anything and everything] they may ask, it will come to pass and be done for them by My Father in heaven." (Matthew 18:19)

Prayer of agreement carries tremendous power. One kind of prayer settles matters where all else have failed. Known unto Apostles Paul, it's this privilege and potency of prayer he wrote to the Romans " Now I beg you, brethren, that through the Lord Jesus Christ, and through the love of the Spirit, that you strive together with me in prayers to God for me..." (Romans 15:30) To the Corinthians, he wrote, "you also helping together in prayer for us, that thanks may be given by many persons on our behalf ..." (2 Corinthians 1:11) From the Ephesians, he also demanded prayers (Ephesians .6:18-19) To the Thessalonians he wrote about his prayer to them (1 Thessalonians 1:1-2) From the Colossians he demanded prayer partnership for effective ministry. (Colossians 4:3)

Elements in the Prayer of Agreement

1. Agreement about supplication. Therefore, clarity is essential.

2. There must be a common ground on which to stand on; for example, praying in the name of Jesus. "Where two or three are gathered in my name, there am I in them."

3. Answers to prayers are guaranteed and secured. "I say unto you ...it shall be done for them of my father which is in heaven."

4. There is result with better and greater rewards. (Leviticus 26:8; Ecclesiastes 4:9)

Who can pray the Prayer of agreement?

- Husband and wife.

- Friends.

- Any two people either in a team or church gathering.

PRAYER OF SUPPLICATION

"Be careful for nothing; but in everything by prayer and supplication with thanksgiving let your requests be made known unto God." (Philippians 4:6)

SUPPLICATION is:

1. Appeal made to somebody in authority.

Supplication is a humble and sincere appeal to somebody with the power to grant a request.

2. Addressing requests:

The addressing of humble and sincere appeal to somebody with the power to grant them

Who needs this?

- For ourselves, for material, and spiritual matters. (Philippians 4:6)

- For all believers. (Ephesians 6:18)

- For all leaders, spiritual and secular. (1 Timothy 2:1-2)

Examples of supplications:

- Demand for laborers. (Matthew 9:37 -38)

- Requesting for rain of God's spirit. (Zechariah 10:1)

- Praying for forgiveness. (Daniel 9)

- Praying for the spiritual lifting of others. (Ephesians 1:16; Philippians 1:9; Colossians. 1:9; Colossians 4:12)

PRAYER OF INTERCESSION

"And I sought a man among them who should build up the wall and stand in the gap before me for the land that I should not destroy it, but I found none." (Ezekiel 22:30)

"And no one calls on your name and awakens and bestirs himself to take and keep hold of you; for you have hidden your face from us and have delivered us into the [consuming] power of our iniquities." (Isaiah 64:7)

What Is Intercession?

- It is the act of pleading on somebody's behalf.

- It is the attempt to resolve the conflict.

- It is the action of attempting to settle a dispute.

To intercede means to

- To plead with somebody in authority on behalf of somebody else, especially somebody to be punished for something.

- To speak for somebody:

- To speak to support somebody involved in a dispute. Mediate in a dispute.

Examples of People Who Intercede

1. Abraham. (Genesis 18:16-33)

Why Is Intercession Necessary?

➢ To pray for salvation. (Ezekiel 33:11; 22:30-31)
➢ To intercept an impending judgment. (Numbers 14:11-19)
➢ To uphold judgment. (Exodus 32:7-14; Psalm.106: 23)
➢ In intercession the knowledge of God's will is important.

PRAYER OF FAITH

"And Jesus answered them, Truly I say to you, if you have faith (a firm relying trust) and do not doubt, you will not only do what has been done to the fig tree but even if you say to this mountain, be taken up and cast into the sea, it will be done.

"And whatever you ask for in prayer, having faith and [really] believing, you will receive." (Matthew 21:21-22)

Prayer of faith is prayed when there is a desire for things that cannot be seen in the physical.

It is targeted towards particular desires.

It covers every sphere of need; physical, spiritual, marital, material, emotional, and financial needs (3 John 1:2)

PRAYER OF WORSHIP

Luke 24:52-53; Ephesians 5:18-20; Acts 13:1-4

The church of acts constantly praises, the Lord not singing to entertain themselves but ministering to the Lord (Acts 2:47) Praising God is their lifestyle, not an occasional thing. A watchman that wants to make a mark of distinction cannot do without a lifestyle of praise unto God, regardless of personal discomfort. Paul and Silas were not in a comfort zone when they praised God

As a team also, whenever we call prayer meetings, let's have high praise unto God, not be found wanting. It would have been hard for Silas and Paul if they had not been used to that life.

It releases the atmosphere of miracles, healing, and deliverance. (2 Chronicles 20; Acts 16:25; Psalm 149)

It releases the atmosphere for the manifestations of the gifts of the Holy Spirit. The bible says, "while they were worshipping the Lord and fasting, the Holy Spirit said, separate now for me Barnabas and Saul for the work to which I have called them." (Acts 13 2)

It enables the atmosphere for the supernatural intervention. [2 Chronicles 20]

It enables the atmosphere for divine instructions and guidance in spiritual warfare. (2 Chronicles 20:15,17)

It enables the manifestation of the presence of God. (2 Chronicles 5:12-14; Luke 5:17; Psalm 22:3)

It enables the manifestations of the power of God. (2 Chronicles 20:22-25; Luke 5:17)

UNITED /CORPORATE PRAYER

"And when they heard it, lifted their voices together with one united mind to God and said, O Sovereign Lord, you are He Who made the heaven and the earth and the sea and everything that is in them." Acts 4:24

It is the corporate prayer of over two or three people. It is a prayer that features many people raising their voices simultaneously over the same subject. [Acts 1:14; 2:1]

Corporate prayers involve many people with collective interest, it is sometimes called for when there is urgency or in a time of great need. (Acts 4:12]

It should be done in one accord, but unfortunately, most corporate prayers are hindered because of lack of unity of purpose among those praying. In Corporate prayer, corporate need should be above every other preference. If prayer is raised and you don't buy into it, excuse yourself from that meeting.

The prayer should be specific and show to everyone involved in praying. For example, the disciples prayed, "And now, Lord, observe their threats and grand to your bondservants [full freedom] to declare your message fearlessly." (Acts 4:29)

Corporate prayer or united prayers are catalysts for revival.

It ushers in the power of God to pull down what needs to be pulled down. (Jeremiah 1:10; 2 Corinthians 10:4; 31)

Boldness and courage are released. (Acts 4:31)

The word would be preached with power. (Acts 4:31; 2 Thessalonians 3:1)

United prayer ushers in the glory of God. (2 Chronicles 5:6-7,11-14)

It releases the fire. (2 Chronicles 7:1-3)

PRAYER OF COMMITMENT

"Casting the whole of your care [all your anxieties, all your worries, all your concerns, once and for all] on Him, for He cares for you affectionately and cares about you watchfully." (1 Peter 5:7)

"Be careful about nothing; but with prayer and supplication with thanksgiving let your request be made known unto God." (Philippians 4:6)

It is committing one's needs and problems to God. Jesus gave an invitation in Matthew 11:28 "Come to Me, all you who labor and are heavy -laden and overburdened and I will cause you to rest."

To be effective in this assignment you have to learn how to roll over your issues to God. There will be many challenges, personal and ministerial. Note when it comes because it will come, Jesus Himself told us, "In the world you have tribulation and trials and distress and frustrations; but be of good cheer [take courage, be confident, certain, and undaunted] for I have overcome the world [I have deprived it of power to harm you and have conquered it for you.]" (John 16:33)

A problem does not indicate being out of God's will

and possession, and acquisitions are not marks of acceptance by God. Paul and Silas were in the will of God when they encountered problems that landed them in prison.

Prayer of commitment is a prayer rolling out all worries, cares, and anxieties unto Jesus. (Psalm 37:5; Proverbs 3:5-6; 16:3)

It is a prayer of acknowledgment of God and His ability to do what is requested from Him

It is a prayer of agreement with the word of God. (Psalm 119:89)

When we don't commit our matters unto God, there will be distractions, and lack of focus and the enemy wanted that anyway.

"Therefore then, since we are surrounded by so great a cloud of witnesses [who have borne testimony to the Truth], let us strip off and throw aside every encumbrance (unnecessary weight) and that sin which so readily (deftly and cleverly) clings to and entangles us, and let us run with patient endurance and steady and active persistence the appointed course of the race that is set before us, Looking away [from all that will distract] to Jesus, Who is the Leader and the Source of our faith [giving the first incentive for our belief] and is also it's Finisher [bringing it to maturity and perfection]. He, for the joy [of obtaining the prize] that was set before Him, endured

the cross, despising and ignoring the shame, and is now seated at the right hand of the throne of God." (Hebrews 12:1-2)

Worry and anxiety are sins, and they need to be dropped off.

Prayer of commitment is also a prayer of the pursuit of the determination to pursue God's purpose, rather than a personal agenda. "Let us strip off and throw aside every ..." (Hebrews 11:1) That was what Elisha did before the mantle of Elisha fell on him, (2 Kings 2:12)

Prayer of commitment enables concentration and focus on the godly assignment.

PRAYER OF BINDING AND LOOSING

"Assuredly, I say to you, whatever you bind on earth will be bound in heaven, and whatever you loose on earth will be loosed in heaven." (Matthew 18:18)

It is prayer of warfare whereby captives are released from the dungeons of the Devil. (Isaiah 49:24-26)

It is a prayer to rescue people from the Kingdom of darkness to the marvelous light (Colossians 1:13)

PROPHETIC PRAYING

Prophetic praying is declaring the will of God through His Word over the people of God or situations.

"So [to conclude], my brethren, earnestly desire and set your hearts on prophesying (on being inspired to preach and teach and to interpret God's will and purpose), and do not forbid or hinder speaking in [unknown] tongues."
(1 Corinthians 14:29)

"EAGERLY PURSUE and seek to acquire [this] love [make it your aim, your great quest]; and earnestly desire and cultivate the spiritual endowments (gifts), especially that you may prophesy ([a]interpret the divine will and purpose in inspired preaching and teaching). For one who speaks in an [unknown] tongue speaks not to men but to God, for no one understands or catches his meaning, because in the [Holy] Spirit he utters secret truths and hidden things [not obvious to the understanding]. But [on the other hand], the one who prophesies [who interprets the divine will and purpose in inspired preaching and teaching] speaks to men for their up building and constructive spiritual progress and encouragement and consolation. He who speaks in a [strange] tongue edifies and improves himself, but he who prophesies [interpreting the divine will and purpose and teaching with inspiration] edifies and improves the church and promotes growth [in Christian wisdom, piety, holiness, and happiness]. Now I wish that you might all speak in [unknown] tongues, but more especially [I want you] to prophesy (to be inspired to preach and interpret the divine will and purpose). He who prophesies [who is inspired to preach and teach] is greater (more useful

and more important) than he who speaks in [unknown] tongues, unless he should interpret [what he says], so that the church may be edified and receive well [from it]." (1 Corinthians 14: 1-6)

While praying in tongue is the divine utterance of the will of God in an unknown language, prophetic praying is declaring the will of God in a known language.

"You shall also decide and decree a thing, and it shall be established for you, and the light [of God's favor] shall shine upon your ways." (Job 22:28)

You can make a positive declaration over yourself or others, and places.

PRAYER OF CONSECRATION:

"Saying, Father, if you are willing, remove this cup from me; yet not my will, but [always] yours be done." (Luke 22:42)

It is a prayer of absolute devotion and surrender to the will of God. It is prayed when the will of God is known, but there is struggling to surrender to that will.

It is prayed in demonstrating availability for God's use.

PRAYING IN TONGUES

"Therefore, the person who speaks in an [unknown] tongue

should pray [for the power] to interpret and explain what he says. For if I pray in an [unknown] tongue, my spirit [by the Holy Spirit within me] prays, but my mind is unproductive [it bears no fruit and helps nobody]" (1 Corinthians 14:13-14)

Praying in tongues is prayer uttered in an unknown tongue to the one praying but known to God.

It comes because of the baptism of the Holy Spirit. (Acts 2:14)

It is direct communication with God. (1 Corinthians 14:2)

Praying in tongues enables you to be built up spiritually. It edifies the people praying. (Jude 20; 1 Corinthians 14:4)

It magnifies God. (Acts 10:46)

Praying in tongues is the best form of prayer when prompted by the Holy Spirit to pray for someone or about something, and you don't know what to pray. (Roman 8:26) A name popped in your head during the night, the only option you will have is to first pray in the spirit until there is release or a word.

Sometimes one can pray to the point of the Holy Spirit interpreting what you have prayed about, in your spirit. (Job 32:2) but one thing, you will always know later by manifestations.

Praying in tongue is the open door to the supernatural.

It the best way to pray selfless prayers.

For more understanding of Praying in Tongues. Study 1 Corinthians 14.

Some Essentials:

Prayer moves the hands of God to show his power in any given situation in the visible world. Although prayer does not change God's attitude, it influences his actions.

Through prayer we get into partnership to determine the future, like the Anna and the Simeons of this world, certain things will and certain that are not meant to happen should not happen if we pray rightly.

Regardless of whether God has spoken or not, start no program or project without first praying through.

Before you can win the battle in the physical, you first have to win in the spirit. The spiritual controls the physical.

When prayer is sufficient enough doors are open on their own accord in high places; doors to favor, and resources.

What is gained by prayer must be maintained by prayer.

Don't just talk about prayer, pray. I have seen many prayer conferences where prayer is just taught but not prayed.

Discern what to pray about.

Be specific so you can know if there are answers.

Your prayer must be targeted.

Your prayer must be aggressive.

Your prayer must be empowered by the Holy Spirit.

Your prayer must be intentional.

You must know the enemy's strategies. I once invited military personnel to come train us on military tactics in dealing with the enemy, and it was helpful.

Know there will always be a spiritual counterattack.

Know as Christians we are not immune to Satanic attacks. You cannot afford to trivialize his schemes.

AS A WATCHMAN, HOW DO YOU MEASURE THE EFFECTIVENESS OF PRAYER?

- When you see an increase in concrete, measurable answers to prayers. (James 5: 17-18)

- When the church becomes influential in the city through powerful prayer

- The spiritual controls the physical.

- When violence ceases in the land. (Isaiah 60:18)

- When there is the mass salvation of souls.

- When the economy becomes buoyant.

FASTING AND PRAYER

Fasting may be described as emptying of oneself; it is a way of denying self will, desires, to humble oneself before God. It is abstinence from food, and it is also not limited to food but also from other stuff that supply comfort. One can be led to give up something loved for a period of time to devote oneself to God for a period of time, but the most popular thing is food. It has been observed nowadays but abstains from such things as social media, television, adornment with jewelry or anything else. Fasting is not an option for a watchman that wants to make a difference in their assignment, it is a must, not an option. Some situations will respond more effectively with the force of prayer and fasting combined; you can see how Jesus expressed the fact with the story of the demonic boy having noticed the struggle by His disciple in dealing with that issue. There are cases you must deal with that, and they will require prayer and the combination of fasting.

"When they approached the crowd, a man came up to Jesus, kneeling before Him and saying, "Lord, have mercy on my son, for he is a lunatic (moonstruck) and suffers terribly; for he often falls into the fire and often into the water. And I brought him to Your disciples, and they were not able to heal him." And Jesus answered, "You unbelieving and perverted generation, how long shall I be with you? How long shall I put up with you? Bring him here to Me." Jesus rebuked the demon, and it came out of him, and the boy was healed at once.

Then the disciples came to Jesus privately and asked, "Why could we not drive it out?" He answered, "Because of your little faith [your lack of trust and confidence in the power of God]; for I assure you and most solemnly say to you, if you have [living] faith the size of a mustard seed, you will say to this mountain, 'Move from here to there,' and [if it is God's will] it will move; and nothing will be impossible for you. [But this kind of demon does not go out except by prayer and fasting.]" (Luke 17:14 -21)

Why Do We Have to Fast?

Fasting will help us to position our hearts and minds in the right frame to recognize when and how we have gone astray and to run to the merciful arms of God (Joel 2) We have Fasting, which makes a prayer life more vibrant, effective, and efficient. Not all prayer works but effective prayer does

Fasting empowers prayer. (Matthew 17:21)

Fasting sustains prayer life. We were told Anna who prayed the Messiah into existence engaged in regular fasting and prayer. (Luke 2: 36 - 37)

To know the will of God in any particular situation. (2 Chronicles 20)

Supernatural power

"And I set my face to the Lord God to seek Him by prayer and supplications, with fasting and sackcloth and ashes;" (Daniel 9:3)

"But as for me, when they were sick, my clothing was sackcloth; I afflicted myself with fasting, and I prayed with head bowed on my breast." (Psalm 35:13)

"Then I proclaimed a fast there, at the river Ahava that we might humble ourselves before our God to seek from Him a straight and right way for us, our little ones, and all our possessions." (Ezra 8:21)

"So, we fasted and besought our God for this, and He heard our entreaty." (Ezra 8:23)

"While I was speaking and praying, confessing my sin and the sin of my people Israel, and presenting my supplication before the Lord my God for the holy hill of my God. Yes, while I was speaking in prayer, the man Gabriel, whom I had seen in the former vision, being caused to fly swiftly, came near to me and touched me about the time of the evening sacrifice. He instructed me and made me understand; he talked with me and said, O Daniel, I am now come forth to give you skill and wisdom and understanding. At the beginning of your prayers, the word [giving an answer] went forth, and I have come to tell you, for you are greatly beloved. Therefore, consider the matter and understand the vision." (Daniel 9:20-23)

As a watchman, observe weekly scheduled of fasting.

Manners of Fasting

1 Day of Fasting

> ➢ For self-evaluation (Leviticus 16; Psalm 139:23-24)
> ➢ Spiritual warfare (Judges 20)
> ➢ Deliverance (Psalm 109)

1-3 Days of Fasting

> ➢ For mercy over judgment (Daniel 9)
> ➢ For healing (Psalm 35:19; Joel 2)
> ➢ For covering, protection, and preservation (Esther 4)

21 Days of Fasting

> ➢ For revelations (Daniel 10)

40 Days of Fasting

> ➢ For spiritual empowerment (Matthew 4)

THE RETREAT OF A WATCHMAN

If quiet time is a daily spiritual need, then sometimes, a longer stretch of solitude may be needed. For that, there is the 'retreat'. This is done by going to a specific place away from where you live and work, away from hobbies and duties, families and habits, media and pressures. It can be done alone, or with just a spiritual director or sponsor, or with a small group of people with a common purpose or bond. It works because it separates you from life as you know it for more than just a few minutes a day. This gives you a step outside of your entire way of life for a little while and sees it from a different angle. The retreat time can help you get back in touch with parts of yourself that had been bypassed in daily life for efficiency or to avoid the pain. It can be a time of extended discussion with God, of throwing forth thoughts and feelings, working things out, being still, and waiting on the Lord. A retreat may well refresh you with quiet rest, but if that's all the 'retreat' is, then it's just another vacation. The spiritual retreat is time spent with God. It tunes your heart to the Heavenly channels to be able to hear God with precision and accuracy.

TEAMWORK

"I have posted watchmen on your walls, O Jerusalem: they will never be silent day or night. You, who call on the lord, give yourselves no rest." (Isaiah 62:6)

As we can see from Isaiah 62:6 the assignment was not given to one person but several people who needed to work together to accomplish the purpose of God for Jerusalem, which could stand for the Church, family, or a community. Teamwork is part of every organization; we are expected to be a functional part of a performing team. A strong team is to the benefit of any organization including a church setting.

All watchmen cannot be boxed in one box, for not all have the same burden, passion, or style. Due to unique personality traits and gift mix, the team leader must know how to effectively mobilize and deploy watchmen to different watches.

It is also essential too for the individual to know their burdens, passion, and style; and learn how to work in a team for achieving a corporate goal.

For the teamwork to be effective, there is a need for certain protocols to be established by whoever is leading a team or any particular prayer meeting.

- Establish a goal for the meeting.

- Communicate the goal to the participant.

- Call for the leading and help of the Holy Spirit.

- Diversities in calling and the gift should be embraced rather than despised.

- The leader should control diversions or shift from established goal.

- Prayers may be done in diverse ways, but there should be maintenance of "one sound" (2 Chronicles 5:13;1 Corinthians 14:8)

- Corporate goal should be above self.

- The leader should protect the meeting from being hijacked by such who intimidate, monopolize or manipulate.

BUILDING THE WATCH

"I have posted watchmen on your walls, O Jerusalem: they will never be silent day or night. You, who call on the lord, give yourselves no rest". (Isaiah 62:6)

The essence of prayer WATCH is to ensure there is around the clock ongoing prayer with a purpose. (Leviticus 6:13) According to Cindy Jacobs, "A prayer watch may take a variety of lengths and forms. Some churches have "prayer lock-ins" in which a group stays in the church building in prayer all night long. In other churches, people come on a 24-hour rotational basis." In my church, Jesus House Chicago we do have a 24-hour prayer lock-in called Prayer-thon. It usually runs for between 3-5 days divided 2-hours slot. The advantage of this kind of prayer watch is that it allows the incorporation of different gift mix and also enables wide coverage.

- The Watch coordinator or the Pastor or both should set the theme for the Watch by the leading of the Holy Spirit.

- The days should be segmented into slots.

- A sign–up sheet should be drawn, and members should be encouraged to sign up based on availability.

- Leaders should be chosen for each slot.

THE WATCHMAN AND THE PRAYER WALK

Prayer walking is a direct way of taking the battles to the field.

"And then the night watchmen found me as they patrolled the darkened city. Have you seen my dear lost love?" (Song of Solomon 3:3, 7)

Sometimes as the Spirit leads, I lead my team to walk around the Church vicinity praying over the community. That is an idea that you would want to adopt since we are not isolated from the community we are at.

EXPECTATION

- As a Watchman, you are expected to be a keeper of people, places, and things against losses.

- As a watchman to be a guard to people, places, and things acting as a shield, an armor, bearer to protect from any external attacks. They are expected to build a wall of protection around the object of the watch.

- As Watchman, you are expected to pose as a gate/doorkeeper keeping vigilant on what comes in and out of place.

- The Watchman is expected to maintain things for the Lord. Though not a vision setter, still maintain the vision. They maintain orders.

- All the above are achieved through the instrument of prayer

- The Holy Spirit should be the person leading, giving direction and strategies.

CHAPTER 7
POSSIBLE PROBLEMS AND SOLUTIONS OF THE WATCHMAN

"The great battles, the battles that decide our destiny and the destiny of generations unborn, are not fought on public platforms, but in the lowly hours of the night and in moments of agony." - Samuel Logan Brengle

SCRIPTURE

"Who is blind but my servant, or deaf as my messenger whom I send? Who is blind as he who is perfect, And blind as the LORD's servant. Seeing many things, but you do not observe; Opening the ears but he does not hear." (Isaiah 42:19 - 20)

The watchman is expected to see, hear, and speak. (Ezekiel 33:6-7) There would be a problem if the watchman is blind so he cannot see beyond the physical or cannot even hear what God is saying. Eli at a time became a deaf watchman, so God had to speak through a much younger person, Samuel to convey a message to him. Jesus also observed problems in His disciples:

"Then Jesus went with them to a place called Gethsemane, and He told His disciples, sit down here while I go over yonder and pray. And taking with Him Peter and the two sons of Zebedee, He began to show grief and distress of mind and was deeply depressed. Then He said to them, my soul is very sad and deeply grieved, so that I_am almost dying of sorrow. Stay here and keep awake and keep watch with me. And going a little farther, He threw Himself upon the ground on His face and prayed saying, My Father, if it is possible, let this cup pass away from Me; nevertheless, not what I will [not what I desire], but as You will and desire. And He came to the disciples and found them sleeping, and He said to Peter, What! Are you so utterly unable to stay awake and keep watch with me for one hour? All of you must keep awake (give strict attention, be cautious and active) and watch and pray, that you may not come into temptation. The spirit indeed is willing, but the flesh is weak. Again, a second time He went away and prayed, My Father, if this cannot pass by unless I drink it, your will be done. And again, He came and found them sleeping, for their eyes were weighed down with sleep. So, leaving them again, He went away

and prayed for the third time, using the same words. Then He returned to the disciples and said to them, are you still sleeping and taking your rest? Behold, the hour is at hand, and the Son of Man is betrayed into the hands of specially wicked sinners whose way or nature it is to act in opposition to God]. Get up, let us be going! See, my betrayer is at hand! As He was still speaking, Judas, one of the twelve [apostles], came up, and with him a great crowd with swords and clubs, from the chief priests and elders of the people.

Now the betrayer had given them a sign, saying, The One I shall kiss is the Man; seize Him. And he came up to Jesus at once and said, Hail (greetings, good health to You, long life to You), Master! And he embraced Him and kissed Him with [pretended] warmth and devotion. Jesus said to him, Friend, for what are you here? Then they came up and laid hands on Jesus and arrested Him." (Matthew 26: 36 -50)

"Israel's watchmen are blind, they are all without knowledge; they are all dumb dogs, they cannot bark; dreaming, lying down, they love to slumber Isaiah Hear, you deaf! And look, you blind, that you may see! Who is blind but my servant [Israel]? Or deaf like my messenger whom I send? Who is blind like the one who is at peace with me [who has been admitted to covenant relationship with me]? Yes, who is blind like the Lord's servant? You have seen many things, but you do not observe or apprehend their true meaning. His ears are open, but he hears not!" (Isaiah 42:19 -20)

"And I will bring the blind by a way that they know not; I will lead them in paths that they have not known. I will make darkness into light before them and make uneven places into a plain. These things I have determined to do [for them]; and I will not leave them forsaken." (Isaiah 42: 16)

The watchmen are not exempted from problems. There are possible problems of a watchman and solutions to overcome these problems. The following are the problems of the Watchman.

- **Blindness:** The watchman must see, if he is blind there would be nothing to declare according to Isaiah 21:6. A watchman must have spiritual insight.

"For thus has the Lord said to me: Go, set yourself as a watchman, and let him declare what he sees." (Isaiah 21:6)

- **Deafness:** To speak to the people of God you must be able to spend much more time in the presence of the God of the people to hear him (1 Peter 4:11)

"Son of man, I have made you a watchman to the house of Israel; therefore, hear the word at my mouth and give them warning from Me. A watchman must be able to hear from God and pass on the Instructions to those that he is watching over." (Ezekiel 3:17)

- **Dumbness:** A watchman should not be dumb. As a watchman you have be bold to speak out on what you hear from God just like Paul prayed, "And for me, that utterances may be given to me, that I may open my mouth boldly to make known the mystery of the gospel .... that in it I may speak boldly, as I ought to speak." (Ephesians 6: 18 -20)

A watchman needs to be smart to things to do his/her task effectively.

- **Secret Sins:** There can be no sin hidden from God, but we can hide our sins from fellow humans in pretending to be what we are not and getting involved in what we are not supposed to be doing, especially when it is obviously a sin. The story of Joshua the high priest in the book of Zechariah 3 is of particular interest. He would always minister to God on behalf of the people but was stopped in his track one day as he was going again by the accuser of the brethren. The moral of the story is that as a watchman, stay away as much as you can from living in sin. (Psalm 68:18; Isaiah 59:1-2; Proverbs 15: 8,29; Psalm 25; 24: 3-4)

- **Harboring Unforgiving Spirit:** Unforgiving spirit is one problem of a watchman. A watchman with an unforgiving spirit will always be hindered from entering into the presence of God, which will eventually lead to unanswered prayers. (Mark 11:25-26)

- **Unresolved family conflicts:** A watchman cannot afford to have problems or conflict with his/her family members. A watchman should always be at peace with his or her husband or wife. (1 Peter 3:6-7)

- **Self-defense:** A watchman must have a lot of wisdom and understanding to know when to fight and when not to. God is always there to take revenge on our enemies, we need not defend ourselves all the time. There are certain things we just have to overlook. In the book of Luke 22:26 Jesus tells his remaining disciples, if you have no sword, sell your cloak and buy one. Jesus knew that it was almost his time to be taken and his disciples would be threatened. After a short while, Jesus is arrested, and Peter took a sword to cut off someone's ear to defend Jesus. Jesus rebuked him because he was standing in God's will. Therefore, a watchman must have a lot of wisdom and understanding to know when to fight and when not to. (2 Chronicles 15:2-26)

- **Lack of mercy:** The watchman must always display and extend mercy to others. Lack of mercy is one problem of a watchman. A watchman cannot perform properly if he doesn't exhibit mercy towards people at large, besides those that he/she prays for. You need the mercy of God, so you must also extend mercy to others. To show mercy, you must avoid being judgmental. Don't take sides with the accuser of the brethren against the people whom you are praying for. (Proverbs 21:13; Matthew 5:7; Isaiah 11:3)

- **Hypocrisy:** Hypocrisy is not a good attribute for a watchman. Hypocrisy for a watchman is a situation when a watchman pretends to be what he is not. An example is to pretend to the team you are praying when you are not. (Matthew 6:5)

People who practiced hypocrisy in the bible were called by many names such as; Hypocrites, pretenders, play actors, false persons.

Hypocrisy is feigning to be what you are not.

- Don't pretend to be what you are not.

- Don't act with the grace you don't have. David did not pretend to know how to use Saul's weapon. (1 Samuel 17)

- Don't pretend to be holier than you are, we are all work in progress. (Matthew 15:7; 7:5; Matthew 6:5)

Consequences of Hypocrisy

- Punishment awaiting such a person. (Matthew 24:51)

- Greater condemnation. (Matthew 23:14)

- **Distractions:** Distractions are not good for a watchman. As a watchman, we must be able to be the focus and concentrate on the things of

God allowing no distraction from out there us. (2 Kings 2:2-16; Luke 10: 38-42; Hebrews 12:1-2)

- **Impatience:** Impatience is not a good quality for a watchman. A watchman needs to be patient with people we pray for any everyone around us. We need to be patient in doing the will of God and in receiving the promises of God and hearing from God. Patience is the fruit of faith. (Hebrews 10: 35 -36)

"Whoever is patient has a great understanding, but one who is quick-tempered displays folly." (Proverbs 14:29)

- **Self-dependence:** Self-dependence is not proper for a watchman. As watchmen, we must not depend on ourselves but on God who is the author and finisher of our faith.

"Not that we are competent in ourselves to claim anything for ourselves, but our competence comes from God." (2 Corinthians 3:5)

- **Pride:** Pride is arrogant or disdainful conduct or treatment of other people. It is an attitude of haughtiness and a feeling of superiority. The proud have an excessive and high opinion of one's self. Pride is conceit. People who are proud see other people and things around them as beneath them. Pride has contempt for things and people. The proud exhibits vanity. The proud flaunts achievements and accomplishments. (Proverbs 16:18)

A watchman should take no glory to his/herself. All glory must be unto the lord. The sin of pride is one problem of the watchman.

"For everything in the world—the lust of the flesh, the lust of the eyes, and the pride of life-comes not from the father but from the world." (1 John 2:16)

It will be hard for proud people to work with a team, they are actually team breakers.

Symptoms of Pride

- Appropriating God's glory to oneself. (Isaiah 42:8)

- Reliance on self. (Hosea 5:5)

- Failure to inquire of the Lord before embarking on any exploits no matter how minimal. (Hosea 7:10)

- Controversial. (1 Timothy 6:4)

- Rudeness and rebellion to constituted authority. (1 Corinthians 13:5)

- Desire to having one's way most of the time. (1 Corinthians 13:5)

- Desire to lord it over others that is a manifestation of 'Jezebel 'spirit.

- Discontentment with the placed position.

- Self-seeking.

- Self-exaltation.

- Unforgiveness.

Results of Pride

- Makes you become a byword. (Ezekiel 16:56)

- Makes you unprofitable in your calling. (Jeremiah 13:9-10)

- Pride brings fight and contention. (Proverbs 13:10; 1 Timothy 6:4)

- Pride will bring you low. (Proverbs 29:2; Matthew 23:12; Daniel 4:37)

- Fruitless efforts in ministry due to close heaven. It results in unanswered prayers. (Leviticus 26: 19-20; Matthew 3:16-17)

- Emptiness. Proverbs 11:2

- Pride is a destroyer.

God hates pride. In Proverbs 6:16-19, God listed seven things which He hates in pride. It was recorded in James 4:6, "God resists the proud, but gives the grace to the humble."

Without the grace, service to God in any capacity becomes hard. Grace differentiates a successful minister from the rest. (1 Corinthians 15:10)

- Pride deprives you of grace, which grants you divine ability to do what ordinarily you could not do. God knew it would be difficult to do and that is why He promised to release the spirit of grace.

"And I will pour out upon the house of David and on inhabitants of Jerusalem the Spirit of grace and supplication." (Zechariah 12:10)

Dealing with Pride

- Having the mind of Christ. (Philippians 2:5)

- Have a modest opinion of yourself. (1 Peter 5:6; Galatians 6:3; Romans 12:3)

- Learn how to appreciate and work with others.

- Don't put people down.

- Be quick to forgive.

- Do not be susceptible to offenses.

- Always appropriate glory to God.

- Do not be self-promoting or self-ambitious.

- Do not be eager for recognition or reward.

- Study, memorize, and walk in the word. (Psalm.119:9; Joshua 1:8; John 13:34)

- The more God is using you, the more you should run from pride. The more you surrender to Him the more height He will take you.

- **Ingratitude:** A watchman that is ungrateful cannot receive more from God. You may not know how to sing, but you must know how to appreciate and worship God. It is to your advantage; God dwells in praise of His people. And praise brings increase. (Psalm 92 :1; 22: 3; 67: 5-6)

CHAPTER 8
THE PROTECTION FOR THE WATCHMAN

"O, do not pray for easy lives. Pray to be stronger men. Do not pray for tasks equal to your powers. Pray for powers equal to your tasks." - Phillips Brooks

SCRIPTURE

"But you [Jeremiah], gird up your loins [in preparation]! Get up and tell them all which I command you. Do not be distraught and break down at the sight of their [hostile] faces, or I will bewilder you before them and allow you to be overcome. Now behold, I have made you today like a fortified city and like an iron pillar and like bronze walls against the whole land—against the [successive] kings of Judah, against its leaders, against its priests, and against the people of the land [giving you divine strength which no hostile power can overcome].

They will fight against you, but they will not [ultimately] prevail over you, for I am with you [always] to protect you and deliver you," says the Lord." (Jeremiah 1:17-19)

Although it was God sending Jeremiah on assignment, he was still expected to face oppositions and hostilities, but he was prepared and equipped for it. May I at this point let you know that the assignment of Watchmen is not bread and butter, or an easy task, but one full of challenges. May I also tell you God got your back. From my own experience, there are days of crying, giving up, discouragement, due to oppositions and hostilities, especially when it comes from the very people you're standing in gap for. And like Apostle Paul attested, "Who shall separate us from the love of Christ? Shall tribulation, or distress, or persecution, or famine, or nakedness, or peril, or sword?... Yet in all these things we are more than conquerors through Him who loved us." (Romans 8 35 -37) So, no matter what comes up in your assignment, you are more than a conqueror. Don't look back, don't look down, only look up, to the author and the finisher of your faith, who called you and who is also faithful to protect you.

That is, the protection for the watchman is very important. The watchman must also watch over his/herself and be protected from the devices of the enemy roundabout. One of the major ministries that the enemy targets is the watchmen ministry because of how delicate their responsibilities are.

Therefore, a watchman must be able to:

KNOW THE ENEMY

As a Soldier in the army of the Lord, you must possess military intelligence.

- Knowing the enemy.

- Knowing how he operates.

- Knowing his goals and objectives.

- But also know your authority, strength, weapons, and power.

We need to know, "So that Satan will not outsmart us. For we are familiar with his evil schemes." (2 Corinthians 2:11)

John 10:10; Ephesians 6: 10-18; 2 Corinthians 10:4; 1 Peter 5:8-9

FALLACIES TO WATCH OUT FOR AND AVOID

You need to know and avoid these pitfalls, so you don't enter and operate in error that could lead to spiritual destruction and ministry reproach.

- **DEMON CONSCIOUSNESS:** Don't give too much attention to Satan. Devil is not responsible for every challenge we go through or circumstances around us, some things are due to our carelessness or ignorance. Do not attribute all power to the Devil, he is not all powerful, he is not omnipresent or omniscient, our God is.

- **OVEREXAGGERATING THE IMPORTANCE OF DEVIL:** Satan's importance is over exaggerated when we attribute the power he does not have to him, comparing him to God. Don't ever think that things happen because he knew about it. Don't appropriate to him the power he does not have.

- **OVER SPIRITUALIZING MATTERS:** Don't explain everything in spiritual terms. I always tell my team, be discerning not suspecting. Suspicion leads to fear, criticism, and judgment. You will also be looked at as spooky, and your ministry will attract rejection from others. I particularly remember a situation that happened to me some time ago whereby unknown to me I had some spoiled food remnant in my house which attracted flies, but before I could discover that, someone was quick to jump to a conclusion it was caused by the devil. I still chuckle any time I remember the story.

- **PRETENSES:** Avoid false alarm, vision, and travailing or burden. It is a turn-off. This could be a false groaning that distracts from the main meeting.

- **ISOLATION:** Don't stay away from people under the guise of private prayer; it could lead to loneliness. Avoid as much as possible to be a lone ranger. It may also be an indication of untreated pride.

- **SUPERIORITY COMPLEX:** Superiority complex: There must be submission at a certain level. As a watchman, you should not submit to the authority of another person who is not submissive to the leadership of a local church.

- **REBELLIOUS ATTITUDE:** You cannot be a watchman and be critical of your Pastor, your assignment is to pray for him. Beware of joining the unhappy party in the church.

- **WOUNDED SPIRIT:** Avoid ministering with hurt. Hurt happens when an intercessor is misunderstood and misinterpreted and therefore suffers abuse; especially from the leadership of a church. A watchman needs spiritual coverage from a local pastor. It would be dangerous if he or she cannot get one; that would be an opening to the enemy's attack, not just on the watchman but on the whole church. I discovered that if the enemy cannot get through the watchman to attack the church, they can go through an undiscerning pastor. One major weapon is the ministry of lying. A natural reaction of the wounded intercessor is to be angry, manipulate others to join her party and become critical of the church leadership. I will advise, if you get into that trap, to stop ministering and deal with your wounds first.

- **WITCHCRAFT PRAYING:** Witchcraft praying is praying out of God's revealed will. It is manipulative and biased. Be careful that your interest is not clashing against God's. To be safe, always pray the scripture and not your desire or opinion over others. An example of such prayer is, "O Lord, deal with my pastor who has become stubborn, let him be broken." That is controlling and manipulative. The spirit of witchcraft is the spirit of manipulation. It also sounds like reporting and judging. It would have been better to pray this way. "Father let your grace abound to my pastor in every area and grant unto him wisdom from above." (James 1:5)

WHAT SHOULD YOU DO?

- **Draw closer to God and continually seek Him daily.** Besides standing in gap or praying for others, always have moments with God and periodic time for personal consecration through prayer and fasting; I will suggest a weekly schedule of waiting on God. (James 4:8; Ephesians 5:18; 1 Peter 1:1-25; Leviticus 21:21; Psalm 145: 18; Hebrews 10:22; 2 Chronicles 15:2; Psalm 46:7)

- **Draw closer to the Word.** (2 Timothy 3:16 -17; Psalm 119:105; Joshua 1:8; Hebrews 4:12; Psalm 119 :18; 1 Peter 2:2; Psalm 1:2; Job 23:12; Psalm 119)

- **Draw nearer to others.** (1 Corinthians 10:16; Hebrews 3: 12 -14; John 13:34 -35; Romans 12:18; Colossians 3:5,8 -9,12, 13; Genesis 2:18; Ecclesiastes 4:9)

SPIRITUAL COVERING:

GOD IS YOUR COVER! (Psalm 91:1-2; 27:1-3)

Yes, God is your cover, but you also still need human covers; spiritual covering is being under the leadership and spiritual authority of another Christian believer. The validity of your ministry in the eyes of God is spotted by direct submission to a specific person. This could be a pastor or any higher authority in a local church, a more mature Christian or any authority figure.

As a Christian and more so as a Watchman, you are not only accountable to God but also to the leaders in your Church. The cover here could also be the leader of your team or any mature and trusted Christian.

A spiritual cover is expected to be an intercessor in the life and the ministry of the watchman. I am sorry to say this, a person who cannot pray more should not be your spiritual cover. Sometimes a pastor of a local church may not fit into that category in time. If it happens seek the face of God and move out of that terrain, or else it could be injurious to your spiritual and total well-being.

What I suggested to the team I led for 13 years is that the group praying a day after should stand in gap for the current group that is, the Tuesday group should pray for the Monday group and so on.

The Ultimate cover is the Most High God, "He who dwells in the secret place of the Most High shall abide under the shadow of the Almighty." (Psalm 91:1) God is our defense, protection, and shield.

Just like Pastors, intercessors also need Armorbearers. It is suggested if you have extended period of prayer over a particular matter, especially issues relating to spiritual warfare, ask God for armor bearers like Jesus looked for from the company of Peter, James, and John. He has put some armor in place for your protection and defense.

1.The Blood of Jesus. Always appropriate the power in that blood over your life, environment, and circumstances. (Revelations 12:11; Romans 5:9; Ephesians 1:7; 1 John 1:7; Leviticus 17:11; Luke 22:20; Hebrews 12: 24)

2. The Anointing. Another weapon for our protection and defense is the anointing. (Exodus 29:7; Psalm 45:7; 1 Chronicles 16:21-22; 2 Corinthians 1:21-22; 1 Chronicles 16:13; Isaiah 59:19; Psalm 23:1-6; Psalm 89:20 -30; 105: 13 -15)

3. His Presence. The Presence is also protection and defense for the watchman. (Isaiah 43: 1 -4; 41:10; Acts 10:38; Zechariah 2:5; 2 Thessalonians 3:3; Deuteronomy 31:6; Psalm 5:11; 46:157:1 138:7; 1 Thessalonians 5: 23 -34; 2 Samuel 22:3-4

CHAPTER 9
THE PROFIT TO THE WATCHMAN

"Profitability is a shallow goal if it doesn't have a real purpose, and the purpose has to be share the profits with others." - Howard Schultz

SCRIPTURE

"For God is not unjust so as to forget your work and the love which you have shown for His name in ministering to [the needs of] the saints (God's people), as you do." (Hebrews 6: 10)

In every labor, it is said *"there is profit."*(Proverbs 14:23) Just like any other service in the Kingdom, the WATCHMAN service has rewards attached to it. Go see, God knows, and He surely rewards.

That is why you must never look unto any man for your reward, your focus must always be on God, looking unto man for rewards will only result in disappointment and also shoddy service.

"Whatever you do [whatever your task may be], work from the soul [that is, put in your very best effort], as [something done] for the Lord and not for men, knowing [with all certainty] that it is from the Lord [not from men] that you will receive the inheritance which is your [greatest] reward. It is the Lord Christ whom you [actually] serve." (Colossians 3:23 -24)

One thing that inspires a person to respond to any call is to know the reward attached to it. David, our case study, asked what the reward was to be if he could bring Goliath down

"Then David spoke to the men who were standing by him, "What will be done for the man who kills this Philistine and removes the disgrace [of his taunting] from Israel? For who is this uncircumcised Philistine that he has taunted and defied the armies of the living God?" (1 Samuel 17:26 -27)

Peter also asked Jesus what is in there for them?

"Then Peter answered Him, saying, "Look, we have given up everything and followed You [becoming Your disciples and accepting You as Teacher and Lord]; what then will there be for us?" Jesus said to them, "I assure you and most solemnly say to you, in the renewal [that is, the Messianic restoration and regeneration of all things]

when the Son of Man sits on His glorious throne, you
[who have followed Me, becoming My disciples] will also
sit on twelve thrones, judging the twelve tribes of Israel."
(Matthew 19:27 -28)

Of the truth, there is a reward for faithfulness in service,
believe it, confess it regularly and serve faithfully!

*"Let us not grow weary or become discouraged in doing
good, for at the proper time we will reap, if we do not
give in."* (Galatians 6:9)

*"You shall serve [only] the Lord your God, and He shall
bless your bread and water. I will also remove sickness
from among you. No one shall suffer miscarriage or be
barren in your land; I will fulfill the number of your
days."* (Exodus 23:25-26)

*"Because he set his love on Me, therefore I will save him;
I will set him [securely] on high, because he knows My
name [he confidently trusts and relies on Me, knowing I
will never abandon him, no, never]. "He will call upon
Me, and I will answer him; I will be with him in trouble;
I will rescue him and honor him. "With a long life, I will
satisfy him. And I will let him see My salvation."* (Psalm
91:14 -17)

Finally,

*"Fight the good fight of the faith [in the conflict with evil];
take hold of the eternal life to which you were called, and
[for which] you made the good confession [of faith] in the
presence of many witnesses."* (1 Timothy 6:12)

That like Paul you may say,

"I have fought the good and worthy and noble fight, I have finished the race, I have kept the faith [firmly guarding the gospel against error]. In the future there is reserved for me the [victor's] crown of righteousness [for being right with God and doing right], which the Lord, the righteous Judge, will award to me on that [great] day—and not to me only, but also to all those who have loved and longed for and welcomed His appearing." (2 Timothy 4:7-8)

In conclusion, as a fellow watchman, I trust this book has provided a fresh perspective on your calling and how you can best make a lasting impact and please the MASTER. I pray we shall make it home at the end gloriously and hear the Master say: "Well done, good and faithful servant." SELAH!

HALLELUJAH! TO GOD BE ALL THE GLORY!

ABOUT DAMOLA

Damola Treasure Okenla (DTO) is the author of several Christian and inspirational books, a sought-after inspirational speaker, certified life coach, and transformational prayer strategist. She has dedicated her life to uplifting others and helping her clients grow and develop spiritually.

DTO is also the president and founder of Life Encounters Incorporated, a not-for-profit organization dedicated to self-discovery and recovery through seminars, workshops, and retreats. Her organization, like her books, reflects her passion and mission to advocate spiritual freedom and empowerment of individuals.

Her website **www.damolatreasureokenla.com**

FOLLOW DAMOLA:

https://www.facebook.com/CoachDTO

https://www.instagram.com/coachdto/

https://twitter.com/DTO03

FB Groups

https://www.facebook.com/groups/purposelyempoweredwoman/

https://www.facebook.com/groups/transformationalprayersnetwork/

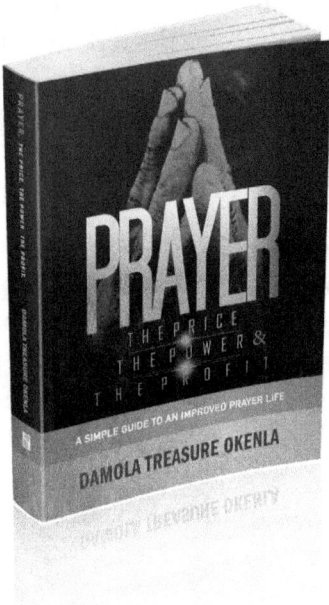

FASTTRACK YOUR FRESH START WITH PRAYER:

A 21-DAY PRAYER JOURNEY

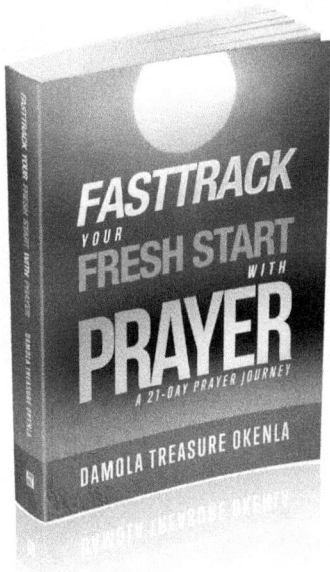

Fresh Start is for those who despite their setbacks in life, are determined to achieve their full potential.

Fresh Start is for people who are ready to push beyond their current challenges or successes because there is always something to be done, to be discovered, to be pursued and captured.

In Fast Tracki Your Fresh Start, Damola Okenla gives a great perspective on a journey that can be done by anyone. You just have to make the choice. She demonstrates the multiple ways you can go about getting yourself back on track with God. If you have lost your way, Damola's inspirational guidance will help you get back on track with faith, hope and confidence.

This 21-day journey is refreshing, and you will not be disappointed in the things you are opened up to and the self-discoveries you are certain to enjoy along the way.

www.ingramcontent.com/pod-product-compliance
Lightning Source LLC
LaVergne TN
LVHW051050080426
835508LV00019B/1797